D1393960

"This easy-to-use guide contains a comprehensive, integrated, systematic approach to developing true teamwork in organizations. It cuts through the fog of current literature on the subject in a refreshing and practical way. **Work Teams That Work** is an excellent resource for human-resources professionals, team leaders, facilitators, supervisors, managers, and executives. If your organization 'does teams,' this is an invaluable aid to their development and continuous improvement."

—John E. Jones, Ph.D., President
 Organizational Universe Systems

"Provides a high-touch approach to reengineering. Results oriented, but never loses sight of the most important element — people.

—Michael W. Wynne, President of Space Systems Division
 General Dynamics Corporation

"A very thorough synthesis of information on team development and a practical reference guide of models and techniques everyone managing or working on a team can use."

—Jim Graham, Director of Sales Training
 R.R. Donnelley & Sons Company

"If self-directed teams are a part of your future strategy, **Work Teams That Work** is a must read for you."

—Ken Blanchard, Author
The One Minute Manager

"**Work Teams That Work** provides teams and leaders an extensive tool-kit filled with the technologies needed to design teams that will thrive in a time of complex and rapid change. In fact, this book is a survival manual for our 'fast-forward,' competitive world. Cross-functional teams are transforming work, breaking old habits and rewriting the rule books. **Work Teams That Work** is essential, simply because it enables us to shape the future."

—Daniel K. Doelger, Ph.D.
Organizational Design and Development Director
Monsanto Chemical Company

"A compilation of all there is to know about the importance of teams in an organization and how members of a team can work together with maximum effectiveness. This is a very useful manual on the dos and don'ts of effective teamwork, presented in highly readable, easily understood, and very specific detail. **Work Teams That Work** will be used and reused in our company."

—George "Bert" Walker, Chairman of the Board
Stifel, Nicholaus & Company, Inc.

"If you are a busy manager or team leader and only have the opportunity to read two books this year, read this one twice. Dr. Montebello has assembled the road map for success in working with individuals and teams."

—Ken Kopelman, Board Secretary
Liz Claiborne, Inc.

"We have used this book as a training tool in the development of cross-functional Product Council teams. As we worked through the chapters, we found the sequence of topics covered was very well laid out. It seemed almost uncanny how the next topics being covered in the book tracked so closely with the areas we happened to be struggling with as our teams developed."

—Tim Lemont, Director of Mining Products
Harnischfeger Corporation

"Growing our business from an entrepreneurship to a professionally managed firm required exceptional teamwork — everyone pulling together to satisfy the needs of our clients. **Work Teams That Work** provided us the means to build strong teamwork and achieve continuous improvements in our business results."

—Bob Jones, President
R.T. Jones Capital Equities, Inc.

"An excellent presentation of the very important team concepts and tools. It is easy to understand and use. It is a book to be used, not just read."

   —Dr. H. James Harrington, Principal
    Ernst and Young

"**Work Teams That Work** is a unique accomplishment in the field of business publications. Montebello has created a practical, step-by-step roadway to team implementation action that is steeped in solid, academic research. This book should be the bible of every organization with a TQM, process reengineering, and organization restructuring initiative underway."

   —Tanya Clemons, Manager,
    Executive & Career Development Staffing & Career Development
    Anheuser-Busch Companies

"This book contains practical tools and techniques every team can and should use. These tools will Zapp! your team."

   —Bill Byham, Author
    Zapp! The Lightning of Empowerment

"In this book, I found excellent discussions of the most common problems (and their solutions) that challenge teams within our organization. Especially valuable was the integration of team effectiveness with process management. We would be much further down the road on our quality journey if we would of had this resource to coach our team leaders from the outset. Montebello has done an excellent job of assembling what you need to know if you're going to lead a team that gets results."

—Douglas W. Rau, Director of Quality
   Pet Incorporated

Work Teams That Work is a super handbook for both organizations and individuals who are serious about developing teams — I wish I'd had this five years ago. This practical handbook is full of models, frameworks, and ready-to-use worksheets any team can readily put to use. I found these tools and techniques were brought alive by the wealth of case examples of how companies have utilized teams to smash traditional organizational boundaries and increase team efficiency and productivity."

—Richard L. Jouett, Director of Training and Staff Development
   Brown Shoe Company

"*Work Teams That Work* equips our people with the skills to work effectively in cross-functional teams, achieve our bold strategic objectives, and navigate the competitive environment of the 90s."

—Bill Baer, Vice President of Human Resources
   GIORGIO Beverly Hills

"Practical and easy to read. A must for everyone in management."

—John Tschohl, Author
Achieving Excellence Through Customer Service

"The importance placed on effective communications, which so many times is overlooked, is a valuable lesson and reminder for all of us in senior line roles. **Work Teams That Work** provides a great road map to improve my management system."

—Gary L. Plummer, Vice President of Field Operations
AgriBank, FCB

"Montebello has created a practical resource loaded with proven methods for increasing work team productivity. We have found the chapter on Managing Productive Meetings to be particularly useful."

—Robert L. Grimm, Vice President of Executive Development
May Department Stores Company

WORK TEAMS THAT WORK

Skills for Managing
Across the Organization

Anthony R. Montebello, Ph.D.

BEST SELLERS
PUBLISHING

Copyright © by Anthony R. Montebello, Ph.D. All rights reserved.
Printed and bound in the United States of America. No part of this book
may be used or reproduced in any manner or form without written
permission from the publisher except in the case of brief quotations in
articles and reviews. For information address Best Sellers Publishing,
9201 East Bloomington Freeway, Minneapolis, MN 55420.
Phone: (612) 888-7672 and Fax: (612) 884-8901.

Publisher's Cataloging in Publication
(Prepared by Quality Books Inc.)

Montebello, Anthony R.
    Work teams that work : skills for managing across the
organization / by Anthony R. Montebello.
    p.   cm.
    Includes bibliographical references.
    Preassigned LCCN: 94-71187.
    ISBN 0-9636268-1-7

    1. Work groups.   I. Title.

HD66.M65 1994   658.4'02
                                       QBI94-731

Table of Contents

Part One...Getting Organized

Part Two...Synergy in Action

Part Three...Tools of the Trade

Acknowledgements

This book started slowly then gained speed. The initial work was born of self-serving interests not dissimilar to Henry Mintzberg's sentiments when he said, "I write first of all for myself. That is how I learn." Devoting an evening here and a weekend there as a learning experience, I soon transformed over 15 years of research and practical experience with teams into a rather voluminous pile of loosely connected chapters. Nothing near a finished book though.

The next stage of my journey began as I sent chapters ahead as pre-reading for business teams I would be consulting with — helping them accelerate the team development process and achieve business objectives like increasing quality, achieving speed, and enhancing customer responsiveness. Positive organization consulting and team training experiences catapulted my motivation to continue with the book to new heights. To see the skills in the chapters come alive and to observe all kinds of teams at all levels quickly develop, over-deliver on business results, and extend heartfelt "thanks" along the way is what spurred me on. And the book began to take shape.

Finally, the staff at Best Sellers provided the encouragement and support I needed to fine tune the manuscript. Their vision along with a lot of attention to detail helped make this book suitable for public consumption.

I extend a sincere thanks to Henry Mintzberg, all the teams I've worked with and learned from over the years, and the people at Best Sellers. All of these people in their own way helped transform a personal learning experience into a well stocked tool kit that provides the array of skills teams and individuals need to manage across the organization. I also owe a special debt of gratitude to Susie and Alison for their patience and permission to retire to the basement periodically to do what I love — write so I can learn and continuously improve my capability to help others develop **Work Teams That Work**.

—A.R.M.

About the Author

Anthony Montebello is an industrial psychologist who has consulted for some of the nation's largest corporations on team-based organization designs and human resource development strategies. He is a Vice President at Psychological Associates, a St. Louis-based international consulting and training firm.

Dr. Montebello has helped improve business results and human resource capabilities in companies like AVON Products, Anheuser-Busch Companies, Bloomingdale's, Brookstone, Brunswick, Emerson Electric, General Dynamics, GIORGIO Beverly Hills, Harnischfeger Industries, Ford Motor Company, ICI Chemical, Liz Claiborne, May Department Stores Company, McDonald's, Mead Paper, Monsanto, National Westminister Banks, R.R. Donnelley, Shell Oil, Standard Chartered Banks, and Ralston Purina.

Before joining Psychological Associates in 1987, Dr. Montebello was Director of Organization Development and Training at a large bank holding company. Prior to that he was a member of the Executive MBA faculty at St. Louis University's School of Business while consulting to organizations in manufacturing, service, and health-care industries.

Dr. Montebello has authored over 50 articles and reviews and is frequently "in press" with research publications on organizational effectiveness and human resource development. His diverse research interests span team-based organization designs, employee selection and development systems, and influence strategies for improving selling and negotiating effectiveness.

Preface

There are literally thousands of books on teams and teamwork, many of which were recently published as executives observed firsthand the tremendous capacity of teams to outperform individuals. Many of these works are academic and scholarly while others are overly simplistic. The intent of *Work Teams That Work* is to provide the practitioner with a comprehensive array of proven skills to develop teams — get them up and running quickly and effectively or provide a needed jump-start to those that have lost their way. This book is for those wanting a handy source of easily referenced techniques for continuously improving teamwork, increasing team member participation and satisfaction, and getting better business results.

Work Teams That Work contains prescriptions and skills to make teams the building blocks of your organization. Gone are the days of the lone ranger — teams are more productive and more fun than working alone. Here's why...

- Bigger, more complex projects can be completed. Teams offer more resources, which means that larger and more complicated projects can be undertaken than can be accomplished by individuals.
- Teams have accountability with authority to achieve better business results. Teams have the wherewithal to provide overall direction to the business process, quickly solve problems, continuously improve operational efficiency, and get stronger bottom-line results.
- Greater creativity and in-depth analysis can be achieved. There are more minds applied to the work and a greater diversity of perspectives brought to bear, which often results in observations and insights that escape the notice of any one individual.
- Improved productivity and quality is the result. Team members stimulate each other, cover for one another, and use each other as sounding boards — all these activities boost the quality of the final product.

It's no surprise that the talk in executive chambers and boardrooms is increasingly focusing on "reengineering," "delayering," and "the horizontal organization." These concepts look great on paper as methods to cut costs, eliminate non-value-adding activities, and promote coordination across the organization around core business processes. Add the human element to the mix and invariably the route to better customer service and higher product quality is dramatically bumpier than anticipated. That's precisely the stimulus that led to *Work Teams That Work* — to enable people with the skills to manage in the team-based corporation.

If you're interested in getting better business results and improving your personal effectiveness, this book is for you. It provides rich case examples of how companies completely dismantled the hierarchy, shed unnecessary work, and achieved major gains in quality, productivity, and efficiency. It provides a proven team development system along with skills and strategies that have been tested, refined, and can be immediately applied to achieve the dual goals of higher productivity and increased satisfaction.

Work Teams That Work is divided into three parts:

Part One — *Getting Organized*, gets teams up and running quickly and productively by helping crystallize team mission, goals, and values that led to the formation of the team in the first place. Experienced teams that can use more direction, organization, and structure should find Part One particularly informative and practical.

Part Two — *Synergy in Action*, provides teams, at any level, with practical techniques to conduct productive meetings, define and coordinate roles, solve tough problems, make sound decisions, manage conflict, and open up communication channels in all directions. These are the skills and techniques essential for synergy — pooling team resources to achieve results that are multiplicative, not just additive of individual members' contributions. The equation "1 + 1 = 3" may look like bad math, but imagine the results your team will get when disruptive conflict becomes productive synergy.

Part Three — *Tools of the Trade*, provides teams with a powerful toolbox that includes methods for planning future opportunities and strategies, techniques for constructing and using practical appraisal processes, strategies for redesigning work and reengineering work flow, and leadership skills for getting results through teams.

Armed with this arsenal of proven skills and techniques, you and your team will quickly exceed the productivity expectations of even your most optimistic supporters. And you'll derive greater satisfaction from working together and seeing the tremendous accomplishments that are possible only through teamwork.

Use the chapters and sections within chapters as stand-alone guides — to be referred to when they are needed and wanted most. Or, proceed through the chapters sequentially — they are arranged logically in a proven sequence to help your team quickly realize its potential and sustain teamwork at high levels.

PART ONE

Getting Organized

Chapter

1ONE

Teamwork and Business Results

"Of the strengths that separate us from other companies, the number 1 thing is our teams and teamwork. We have about 1,900 teams across our group at all levels. Teamwork allows us to accomplish things better than we could do it any other way."
> —Jerry Junkins
>   CEO, Texas Instruments

"Two men working as a team will produce more than three men working as individuals."
> —Charles P. McCormick

Increasing numbers of companies are abandoning the outmoded tradition of dividing work processes into compartmentalized functions and simplified tasks. In these vanguard companies, thinking managers are dismantling unnecessary supervisory structures and empowering teams to enhance quality, improve customer responsiveness, and increase efficiency and productivity. At all levels in many modern organizations, the flat, lean, team-based structures and high-involvement workplaces are being pursued with the urgency of a scavenger hunt.

Why this change? Some argue that loss of competitive market position and changing social values have caused business leaders to rethink how jobs are designed, how functions are organized, and the level of team autonomy. The real reason for this trend toward teamwork is simple: Teamwork works. Companies are discovering that teamwork helps them gain speed, shed unnecessary work, and consistently deliver eye popping gains in productivity, quality, and job satisfaction.

Who would have thought it would be so easy? Organize interdependent work functions and business processes into teams and challenge team members to reach important business objectives like quality or customer service. Give teams autonomy to get things done and team members an opportunity to develop and grow. Provide them with information about how well they're doing. It's a simple matter of trust and belief in people. Companies willing to give it a chance — to close the gap between those who manage and those who work with a more enlightened view of social cooperation — are realizing benefits that exceed their highest expectations.

This chapter is about teamwork — about the trends emerging in workplace innovations and what is envisioned on the horizon. This chapter provides recent case examples to illustrate the positive impact of teams and teamwork on achieving business results. These case studies demonstrate how organizations can vault productivity and efficiency while reducing costs if they are willing to change their ways.

Teams Defined

The word "team" undoubtedly conjures up different images to different people. Some think of sports teams while others envision workplace teams — teams uniting hourly and salaried workers, teams that cut across functional lines, teams on which labor and management collaborate, teams that direct their own activities without supervision.

What do all these teams have in common? McKinsey consultants Jon Katzenbach and Douglas Smith describe a team as follows:[1]

"A team is a small number of people with complementary skills who are committed to a common purpose, performance goals, and approach for which they hold themselves mutually accountable."

The important elements of this definition are *complementary skills, common purpose,* and *mutual accountability.* Without these elements, a team may be little more than a loose collection of individuals with nothing more in common than employment by the same company and a few identical appointments on their calendars.

According to this definition teams are (or should be) everywhere in corporate America. Examples include:

Advice/Involvement Teams
People with relevant experiences and information who identify opportunities for improving work processes or solving problems (e.g., quality circles, employee involvement).

Production/Service Teams
People performing related tasks who coordinate their efforts to produce products or provide services (e.g., autonomous work groups, product/service teams, self managed-work teams, cells, core business process teams).

Special Project Teams
People with special areas of expertise or people who work temporarily on assigned projects aimed at applying innovative ideas or solutions to problems (e.g., task forces, committees).

Functional Teams
People with common functional accountabilities who develop and execute plans, and make and implement operational decisions (e.g., departmental teams).

Individuals Coordinating with Others
Two people who work together on sequential activities within or across functions to complete a partial or whole work process (e.g., internal customer-supplier relationships).

Boss/Direction Report Relationship
Two people working together to achieve mutual goals and continuously improve the performance and potential to assume more responsibility.

Clearly, the applications for teams and teamwork are vast. Unfortunately, the disparity between teams as they are and teams as they could be is also large. Anyone spending much time in what might be called team building will sooner or later conclude Plato was right: The things of this world are very imperfect replicas of the ideas on which they were founded. Many so-called teams in the real world don't work very well. While synergy is the goal (i.e., team output is multiplicative of the individual contributions), some teams produce results that are only additive. Still others produce results that are subtractive — team members would have been better off working alone.

We'll look at the trends toward teamwork and the case examples showing that, for those willing to put forth the effort and energy needed to make them work, the gains in bottom-line results are jaw dropping. In later chapters we'll discuss how to build strong teamwork and high-performing teams.

Teamwork Trends

The use of teams in the American workplace is not new. In the 1920s, a few pioneering companies established problem-solving teams to address issues of quality and efficiency.

What *is* new is the widespread proliferation of teams in American companies. Many believe that teamwork may soon be the norm in United States companies — standard operating procedure.

The American Society for Training and Development asked several hundred human resource executives about teamwork results. Their responses show:
- Productivity "improved" or "significantly improved" in 77% of the companies.
- Quality improvements due to teamwork were reported in 72% of the companies.
- Waste was reduced in 55% of the firms.
- Job satisfaction has improved in 65% of the organizations.
- Enhanced customer service was enjoyed by 57% of the companies.

Additional results reported include more efficient production scheduling and goal setting, and increased ability of team-linked employees to resolve their own disputes.[2]

Executives surveyed in an *Industry Week* survey were equally positive about the benefits of teams. When asked to list the top benefit, improved quality (reported by 30%) headed the list, followed by improved productivity (24%), increased morale (21%), and fewer layers of management (14%).[3]

Reports and statistics published by individual companies support these generalized survey findings. At General Mills productivity in plants using teams is as much as 40% higher than in their traditional plants.[4] The division of 3M that organized around cross-functional teams to develop new products is one of the company's most innovative and fastest growing.[5] Teams at one of Ingersoll-Rand's manufacturing plants reduced scrap in one operation from 15% to 3% and, in another, from 40% to 3%.[6]

Unleashing Employee Talent with the Team-based Organization

Examine manufacturing, product research and development, and service processes in most organizations and you'll find silo-like, compartmentalized functions, fragmented tasks, and simplified activities. Even at white-collar levels, tall vertical structures, with invisible but nearly impenetrable walls, hinder business processes that slice not vertically but horizontally across the organization.

In hierarchical organizations, if there's a festering problem that's bothering the company and its customers, you'll likely find a cross-functional dispute where nobody has control over the whole process. It may be overgeneralizing to say that people who work in different functions hate each other, but these structural barriers must give way to team-based operations if there's to be a company for our sons and daughters to work for.

That's what Xerox did in the design of its new horizontal organization. Xerox was organized functionally with manufacturing, sales, R & D, and the like. The new design literally turned the company on its side, creating nine business processes aimed at market segments such as small companies, office document systems, and engineering systems. Says CEO Paul Allaire: "We've given everyone in the company a direct line of sight to the customer."[7]

Exhibit 1-1 contrasts the horizontal and vertical structures.

In the post-hierarchical era of the 1990s thoughtful executives have found that many work processes are highly complex, nonlinear, and can't be (or shouldn't be) separated into a string of sequential tasks. The work output often requires a high degree of collaboration among individuals, departments, and functions. But as cross-functional disputes get in the way of or dilute coordination and synergistic teamwork, the final result is needlessly delayed or unnecessarily diminished in quality.

Executives vigorously pursuing productivity and quality objectives have concluded that they've overstructured things. By merging previously specialized job functions within work teams, they are gaining both efficiency and effectiveness.

From the Vertical Organization

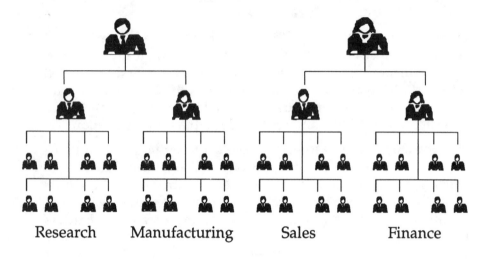

Research   Manufacturing   Sales   Finance

To the Horizontal Organization

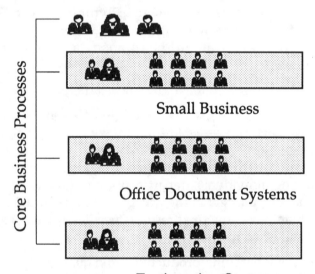

Small Business

Office Document Systems

Engineering Systems

Exhibit 1-1: From Vertical to Horizontal Organization

A case in point. GE Chairman and CEO John F. Welch, Jr., authorized an investigation to find out why other American firms were getting higher productivity growth than GE. He found that companies with the highest sustained growth in productivity focused less on the performance of individual departments and more on how the departments collaborated as products moved among them.[8]

Fragmenting meaningful work processes also robs the people who perform the simplified jobs of self-esteem, a sense of accomplishment, and pride of workmanship.

Commenting on the fact that Kodak production teams do nearly the same amount of work in one shift as they previously did in three, Richard Wilkinson, a supervising engineer at Kodak, cites the more effective use of manpower and *brain power*: "We realized that there was a tremendous resource that was not being tapped."[9]

Workers, from the manufacturing plant to the customer service office, can and want to perform more complex and sophisticated jobs. When given a chance, most have proved they're up to the challenge.

The Competitive Rationale for Teamwork

Teamwork has emerged as the logical approach to sharpening our competitive edge. The reason for the continuing success of teamwork is the focus it places on the human in the job. In a recent article on teamwork, *Business Week* concluded: "American companies are now discovering what the Japanese learned long ago: That people — not technology alone or marketing ploys — are the keys to success in global competition."[10]

GM's NDH Bearings Plant in Ohio is one example. In the early 1980s, jobs were rapidly disappearing as GM outsourced work that had previously been performed in-house. Three product lines were in jeopardy and morale was at an all-time low. When the local UAW threatened to strike, a joint labor-management advisory team was formed to address the issue of work outsourcing.

As a result of negotiations, GM decided to award 80% of a contract for a new, advanced wheel bearing to the Ohio NDH Bearings Plant. In return, GM wanted "reduced manufacturing costs, on-time delivery, and world-class quality." The remaining 20% of the production went to a backup, Japanese producer.

A 14-member team of hourly and salaried NDH plant employees, known as the Synchronous Cell Steering Committee, proposed a major departure from the plant's traditional production process. They reorganized the workflow, redesigned jobs, trained the people — and met all of GM's requirements. When the Japanese failed to deliver its 20% during the first year, NDH produced the additional 20% and subsequently was awarded the entire contract.

Today, scrap in the synchronous cell area is 1.4%, compared to 3.2% for traditional methods of making the same bearings. The unit also boasts the highest machine utilization rate in the plant and inventory levels are 75% lower than those in the rest of the plant. Two plant teams were finalists in a statewide competition for the 1990 Governor's Award for manufacturing excellence. Inspired by this kind of success, management has implemented teamwork elsewhere in the plant; and in the past two years, NDH Bearings has experienced a bottom-line improvement of about 50%.[11]

These success stories are far from unusual as the teamwork initiatives and positive outcomes summarized in Exhibit 1-2 indicate. They suggest the wide range of teamwork applications which are possible in both manufacturing and service firms to achieve important business objectives — improved quality, increased productivity, reduced costs, greater efficiency, enhanced customer service, faster and better product development, and elevated sales.

Company	Team Mission	Results
AT&T Credit Corporation[12]	Cross-functional teams formed to improve efficiency and customer service	Improved productivity (800 versus 400 applications per day) and customer service (decision time on loan approval reduced by 50%)
Federal Express[13]	Clerical teams organized to improve efficiency and customer service	Reduced costs $2.1 million in first year and reduced the number of lost packages and billing errors by 13%
GE Appliances[14]	Production teams organized to reduce manufacturing cycle time by 90% and increase product availability	During first 8 months, reduced cycle time by more than 50% and increased product availability by 6%. Decreased inventory costs by more than 20%
Kodak[15]	Production teams organized to generate ideas about improving the efficiency of operations	Improved productivity (work of 3 shifts now completed in 1)
ORYX Energy[16]	Interdepartmental teams assembled to eliminate unnecessary work	Reduced costs $70 million in a single year
Rubbermaid[17]	Cross-functional teams organized to conduct market research on new products	Increased revenue — sales of new product 50% above projection

Exhibit 1-2: Results from Teamwork Initiatives

Conclusion

Almost without notice, a new and fundamentally different way of managing people is taking shape in American business. Teamwork is replacing the outmoded, adversarial approach that has grown between management and labor and which now threatens the competitiveness of many corporations.

Until recently, work innovations in the United States have progressed slowly. Now the teamwork movement is picking up steam, as evidenced by the statistical and case studies presented in this chapter. Profiting from what was learned from the pioneering efforts, like those at GM's NDH Bearings Plant, hundreds of companies are redesigning work processes, building teamwork, and enjoying the economic and social gains that have for so long been stifled by traditional methods of job simplification and hierarchical structures.

The conclusion here is a simple one: Teamwork works. From a business perspective, teams are more productive, produce higher quality, and are more cost-efficient than solo efforts. From a human relations perspective, the positive effects of teamwork on job satisfaction, motivation, and employee morale have been well documented.

Teamwork is on the rise, and it seems reasonable to project that the number and kinds of companies which use teams as a matter of standard operating procedure will continue to escalate. Companies willing to rethink old ways and apply the lessons learned by forerunners are finding that the payoffs are well worth the investment of time, effort, and expenditure.

Endnotes

1. J.R. Katzenbach & D.K. Smith. *The Wisdom of Teams: Creating the High Performance Organization.* Boston: Harvard Business School Press, 1993.

2. R.S. Wellins & J. George. The Key to Self-Directed Teams. *Training & Development Journal,* April 1991, 26-31.

3. R.S. Wellins, J. Wilson, J.J. Katz, P. Laughlin, C.R. Day, Jr., & D. Price. Self-Directed Teams: A Study of Current Practice. Developmental Dimensions, Inc., Association for Quality and Participation, and *Industry Week,* 1990.

4. B. Dumaine. Who Needs A Boss? *Fortune,* May 7, 1990, 52-60.

5. R.S. Wellins, J. Wilson, J.J. Katz, P. Laughlin, C.R. Day, Jr., & D. Price. Self-Directed Teams: A Study of Current Practice. Developmental Dimensions, Inc., Association for Quality and Participation, and *Industry Week,* 1990.

6. D. Bingham. Calhoun Workers Reach for Responsibility. *Teamwork,* Spring 1991, 6.

7. T. A. Stewart. The Search for the Organization of Tomorrow. *Fortune,* May 18, 1992, 92 - 98.

8. T. A. Stewart. GE Keeps Those Ideas Coming. *Fortune,* August 12, 1991, 41-49.

9. R. Henkoff. Cost Cutting: How to Do It Right. *Fortune,* April 9, 1990, 40-49.

10. J. Hoerr. The Payoff From Teamwork. *Business Week,* July 10, 1989, 56-62.

11. J. H. Sheridan. A Star in the GM Heavens. *Industry Week,* March 18, 1991, 22-26.

12. J. H. Sheridan. A Star in the GM Heavens. *Industry Week,* March 18, 1991, 22-26.

13. R. Henkoff. Cost Cutting: How to Do It Right. *Fortune,* April 9, 1990, 40-49.

14. T. A. Stewart. The Search for the Organization of Tomorrow. *Fortune,* May 18, 1992, 92 - 98.

15. R. Henkoff. Cost Cutting: How to Do It Right. *Fortune,* April 9, 1990, 40-49.

16. R. Henkoff. Cost Cutting: How to Do It Right. *Fortune,* April 9, 1990, 40-49.

17. B. Dumaine. Who Needs A Boss? *Fortune,* May 7, 1990, 52-60.

2wo

Redesigning Work

> *"There will continue to be an emphasis on teamwork as opposed to individual contribution. Hierarchy and authoritarian structures don't involve as many people, so employees don't buy in. And therefore they tend to be less successful."*
>
> —Lawrence Bossidy
> CEO, AlliedSignal

> *"You can play tennis and win a championship and know you've accomplished something. But when you can look in the eyes of your teammates and share that feeling, it's something you can't describe."*
>
> —Brian Trottier
> Pittsburgh Penguins

With increasing urgency companies are leading a march away from the outdated practice of fragmenting jobs into simple, repetitive tasks and closely supervising adherence to detailed rules and procedures. Many organizations are replacing this mode of operating with teamwork.

Employees are no longer being alienated by mindless activities which are vigorously monitored by supervisors wielding awesome disciplinary powers. Rather, teams are being empowered with responsibility and authority to enhance quality, improve customer responsiveness, and increase efficiency and productivity.

This chapter shows how changes in work processes and structures are not only possible, but highly successful. This chapter focuses on how the traditional practice of job simplification has spawned undesirable consequences that no longer fit the realities of today's market and employee expectations. Then it examines the interrelated concepts of job enrichment and teamwork, showing how the dual goals of increasing job satisfaction and improving quality and productivity can be achieved by companies willing to change their ways.

Built-In Obsolescence of Work Simplification

A mechanical engineer, Frederick Taylor (1856-1915), among others, is responsible for the work model that dominated much of worldwide industry throughout most of this century. His concept of "Scientific Management" gave rise to the assembly-line approach to work used in both manufacturing and service organizations at almost every job level.

In the early 1900s, this linear approach to designing work gained widespread popularity. Unskilled labor was abundant. Time-and-motion studies "simplified" tasks which could easily be learned and executed. Because the procedures were simple, mechanical tasks, the training requirements were minimal, and workers were largely interchangeable. The standardized procedures made close supervision easy. Perceived advantages included increased efficiency and the reduced likelihood of errors and quality defects. Although this approach focused myopically on individual efficiency, it served industry remarkably well for many years.

The world of work has changed radically since Taylor's day. Many of our modern manufacturing and service processes aren't linear ones and don't divide tidily into a series of sequential procedures. Even when they do, the efficient operation of tens or hundreds of discrete parts doesn't necessarily translate to overall efficiency and effectiveness of the entire operation. Anyone who has experienced customer-service problems is aware of this fact. Because of technological advances, sophisticated systems such as statistical process control, and increasing demands of customers, work tasks are no longer simple, mechanical gestures. And nearly a century after Taylor, workers are neither unskilled nor uneducated.

Many executives have come to the conclusion that, given today's productivity and quality objectives, they've oversimplified the work process — at every level. By merging previously specialized job functions within work teams, they are gaining both efficiency and effectiveness.

Even when work processes are essentially linear, the efficient operation of all component parts does not necessarily contribute to total efficiency.

It's easy for work activities to get redundant, as Colgate Palmolive discovered when they surveyed managers and their staffs, asking how they spent their workdays. The company found considerable duplication of effort among researchers at different locations and in different departments.[1]

When Hughes Aircraft mapped out every step involved in building a satellite, from design to delivery, they found totally unnecessary actions. Said Joe Sanders, Group Vice President of Operations: "When you stretch it out on the wall like that, things leap out at you. You say, 'What the hell am I doing that for?'" Hughes subsequently pared cycle time from 45 weeks to 22.[2]

Ingersoll-Rand provides an example of improved productivity through interdepartmental teams. Charged with responsibility for improving customer responsiveness, a five-member employee team within the Construction Equipment Group formalized the natural link between parts and service personnel. One of the team's accomplishments was a new system for ordering parts, which saves mechanics a minimum of four hours each day.[3] By combining tasks and empowering teams to accomplish a meaningful business result (improving customer service), workers not only had greater influence over the work process, but they also were more motivated to contribute to organizational goals.

Employees are More Skilled and Better Educated than Most Think

In contrast to Taylor's "typical" worker at the turn of the century, most workers today are highly skilled and well educated. Case in point: Almost every production worker at GM's NDH Bearings Plant in Ohio has at least a high school education; roughly 20% have college degrees; and about 5% have advanced degrees. Glen Resser, business unit director for NDH Bearings, stated: "One of the biggest mistakes I see people make is that they treat their workforce like children."[4]

As Americans have become better educated, the pool of unskilled workers willing to accept oversimplified, mechanical jobs has shrunk. The personal satisfaction they derive from mastering such menial tasks is minimal.

In reality, the tasks that many contemporary workers perform — even on manufacturing assembly lines — are substantially more sophisticated, interesting, and challenging than in the past. As Heinz CEO Anthony J. F. O'Reilly points out, statistical process control and computerized photo-imaging have been added to the carrots-and-peas mix.[5]

Workers have proven that they're up to the challenge. Just three years ago, Kodak production workers operated punch presses eight hours a day. Now organized into teams, the same punch press operators coach fellow team members on mathematical production and quality formulas and help manage just-in-time inventory.[6]

Since the implementation of clerical teams at Federal Express, employees buzz about kaizen — the Japanese concept of continuous improvement — and plot their teams' solutions to complex business problems on sophisticated Pareto charts.[7]

How to Design and Organize Teams

So, what's the best way to form teams so they coordinate like a skillful doubles tennis team — not simply like nine players on a baseball field? The classic Hackman-Oldham Model of job enrichment is perhaps the most useful guide to designing teams, enriching jobs, and organizing work to more efficiently execute important processes and produce higher quality outcomes.[8]

The Model appears in Exhibit 2-1.

It identifies the five basic characteristics inherent, to a greater or lesser extent, in any job:
- *Skill variety* — performing a variety of activities that demand different skills and talents
- *Task identity* — performing a job from beginning to end to produce an identifiable and complete result
- *Task significance* — doing important work that has an effect on others or society in general
- *Autonomy* — freedom and discretion in planning, organizing, scheduling, and performing the work
- *Feedback* — clear and direct information about how well the job is performed

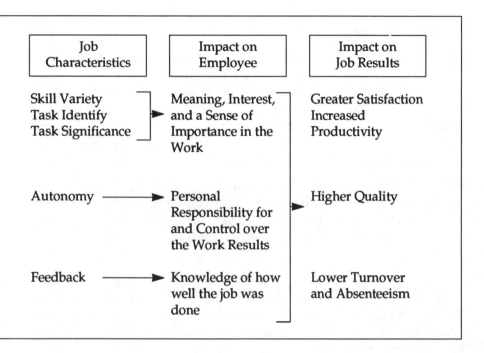

Job Characteristics	Impact on Employee	Impact on Job Results
Skill Variety Task Identify Task Significance	Meaning, Interest, and a Sense of Importance in the Work	Greater Satisfaction Increased Productivity
Autonomy	Personal Responsibility for and Control over the Work Results	Higher Quality
Feedback	Knowledge of how well the job was done	Lower Turnover and Absenteeism

Exhibit 2-1: Job Enrichment Model

Jobs with a high degree of these characteristics motivate workers and consistently deliver jaw-dropping gains in quality and productivity. Teams designed in accordance with these elements organize fragmented, but interdependent, processes into a unit and focus effort on an important business objective such as quality or customer service. Team members are challenged by worthwhile and important job goals that they have control over and are able to determine, on some regular basis, how they are doing. Both human and economic goals are advanced in the process.

Consistent with the job enrichment model, there are three common approaches to forming teams: combining tasks, establishing client relationships, and vertical loading.

Combining Tasks

According to this approach, teams are designed by combining fractionalized tasks to form larger modules (horizontal slices) of work. Larger, more meaningful work is assigned to a team of workers who focus on the business outcomes and, through cross-training, learn all of the component tasks and processes. In doing so, greater skill variety is demanded, along with *task identity* and *task significance.*

An example is the lease processing operation at AT&T Credit Corporation. It appeared to be a fairly straightforward operation: Receive and review applications, check credit standing, notify the applicants of acceptance or rejection, produce contracts, and collect payments.

Several years ago president Thomas C. Wajnert noticed a problem with the division of labor: "The employees had no sense of how their jobs contributed to the final solution for the customer." He combined tasks and formed teams to perform all functions. As a result, applicants received yea-or-nay answers days sooner than before, and the teams processed twice as many applications each day.[9]

Before the change employees described their jobs in terms of activities — receive, review, check, notify. Now the team takes pride in making significant contributions to the organization — extending credit to qualified customers.

Exhibit 2-2 illustrates combining tasks.

Contrast the traditional structure where each department performs a series of discrete tasks with the team structure which organizes around business processes and results. The team mandate is clear and serves as a unifying force for the team. Work is more meaningful, provides greater variety, and the team has control over the resources to produce results vital to the success of the organization.

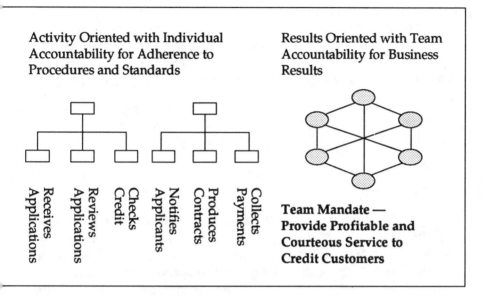

Activity Oriented with Individual
Accountability for Adherence to
Procedures and Standards

Results Oriented with Team
Accountability for Business
Results

Receives Applications
Reviews Applications
Checks Credit
Notifies Applicants
Produces Contracts
Collects Payments

**Team Mandate —
Provide Profitable and
Courteous Service to
Credit Customers**

Exhibit 2-2: Comparison of Traditional to Team Structure
formed by Combining Tasks

Establishing Client Relationships

One consequence of the bureaucratic organization is that workers have little or no power to respond to whoever buys their output — at times someone else in the company. Teams linked to their customers and given the opportunity to suit the people who use their work — not simply whoever cuts their paychecks — realize immediate increases in *skill variety, autonomy* and, most notably, *feedback.*

Teams experience greater skill variety, for example, as they now rely more heavily on interpersonal skills to build and maintain client relationships. They have more autonomy in deciding how to manage the relationship and receive feedback directly from the consumer.

All this spells higher productivity, increased quality, and greater efficiency.

Charged with responsibility for improving customer responsiveness, a five-member interdepartmental team at Ingersoll-Rand formalized the natural link between parts and service personnel. The team devised a new system for ordering parts, saving mechanics a minimum of four hours each day.[10]

By establishing client relationships workers not only have greater influence over the work process, but they also have stronger motivation to contribute to organizational goals.

Vertical Loading

Along with horizontal division of labor, there has been a vertical split between "doing" the work and "planning" and "controlling" the work. Vertical loading calls for delegating to the team responsibilities and controls formerly reserved for management. Usually beginning with simple decision-making activities, greater autonomy to perform responsibilities like hiring, appraising performance, and quality control is delegated as the team develops.

In the case of Kodak production workers, for example, teams have authority to schedule their own work hours and production, inspect their own work, and repair their own equipment. Workers who previously operated punch presses now coach fellow team members, meet with vendors, interview job applicants, and manage just-in-time inventory. More effective use of manpower and brain power enabled this unit to virtually triple its efficiency.[11]

There are scores of tasks that can be transferred from the supervisors to workers to increase the autonomy of teams. Exhibit 2-3 shows a partial listing.

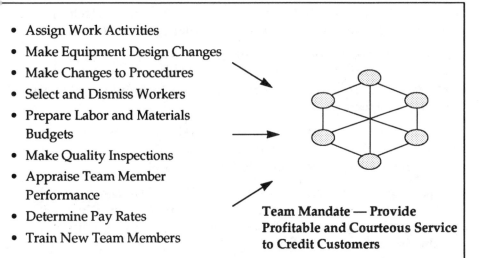

- Assign Work Activities
- Make Equipment Design Changes
- Make Changes to Procedures
- Select and Dismiss Workers
- Prepare Labor and Materials Budgets
- Make Quality Inspections
- Appraise Team Member Performance
- Determine Pay Rates
- Train New Team Members

Team Mandate — Provide Profitable and Courteous Service to Credit Customers

Exhibit 2-3: Vertical Loading of Tasks to Teams

Conclusion

This chapter presented case studies showing major gains realized by companies willing to reorganize work to appeal to new worker values rather than trying to retrofit people to designs of the early 1900s. This chapter also showed how the complexity and interdependency of jobs in most companies competes with attempts to fragment work, simplify tasks, and force worker specialization. If the people element is neglected, or if the complex interrelationship of tasks is not fully considered, companies may compromise important business objectives related to quality, productivity, and customer service.

In addition, this chapter showed the problems with the pervasive practice of job simplification and how attempts to improve efficiency and competitiveness fall short of the mark without accompanying attention to building teams and teamwork. Getting business results through teamwork isn't an overly complicated process. Organize interdependent work functions into teams and challenge team members to achieve important business objectives like cutting costs, enhancing quality, or improving customer service. Give teams autonomy to get things done. And provide them with feedback on how well they're doing. It's a simple matter of trust and belief in people. And companies which have that trust are realizing tremendous social and economic benefits.

A job enrichment model was outlined to explain the impact of work innovations on the all-important human factor — and to provide a guide for managers interested in moving into job redesign and teamwork.

Are the jobs in your organization enriched? What opportunities exist to build teamwork and empower teams with greater responsibility to achieve important business results?

Do your own diagnosis by completing the Job Diagnostic Survey on the following pages. Then take action to get more involvement, better teamwork, and greater job satisfaction tied to quality and productivity.

Job Diagnostic Survey[12]

Respond by circling a number from 1 to 7 indicating how you see your job.

Skill Variety

How much variety is there in your job? That is, to what extent does your job require you to do many different things using many different skills and talents?

1	2	3	4	5	6	7

Very little. The job requires me to do the same routine things over and over again.	Moderate Variety	Very much. The job requires me to do many different things, using a number of different skills.

Task Identity

To what extent does your job involve doing a "whole" and identifiable piece of work? That is, does the job involve an entire work process that has a definite beginning and end? Or does it result in only a small part of the overall piece of work which is finished by others?

1	2	3	4	5	6	7

My job is only a tiny part of the overall work process. The results of my efforts cannot be seen in the final product or service.	My job is a moderate size "chunk" of the work process	My job involves doing the whole piece of work; from start to finish. The results of my effort are easily seen in the final product or service.

Task Significance

In general, how *significant* or *important* is your job? Are the results of your work likely to significantly affect the lives or well-being of other people?

1	2	3	4	5	6	7

Not very significant. The outcomes of my work are not likely to have important effects on others.

Moderately significant.

Very significant. The outcomes of my work affect others in many important ways.

Autonomy

How much autonomy is there in your job? To what extent are you permitted to decide how to go about doing the work?

1	2	3	4	5	6	7

Very little. The job gives me almost no personal say about how the work is done.

Moderate autonomy.

Very much. The job gives me almost complete responsibility for deciding how and when the work gets done.

Feedback

To what extent do you receive feedback about your work performance? Do you get information from supervisors, co-workers, and other sources about how well you are doing?

1	2	3	4	5	6	7

Very little. It is very difficult for me to determine precisely how well I am doing.

Moderate feedback.

Very much. I get almost constant feedback about how well I am doing.

Total Score: _____

ob Enrichment Total Score

	35 —	**Enriched Job**
	34 —	*Little Opportunity to Further*
	33 —	*Enrich Job and Build Teamwork*
	32 —	
	31 —	
	30 —	
	29 —	
	28 —	
	27 —	
	26 —	
	25 —	
	24 —	
	23 —	
	22 —	
	21 —	
	20 —	
	19 —	
	18 —	
	17 —	**Simplified Job**
	16 —	*Significant Opportunity to*
	15 —	*Enrich the Job and Build*
	14 —	*Teamwork*
	13 —	
	12 —	

If your score is 29 or less, you have an opportunity to enrich the job and build teamwork.

Endnotes

1. R. Henkoff. Cost Cutting: How to Do It Right. *Fortune*, April 9, 1990, 40-49.

2. R. Henkoff. Cost Cutting: How to Do It Right. *Fortune*, April 9, 1990, 40-49.

3. S. Goldfarb. Employee Involvement Branches Out. *Teamwork*, Spring 1991, 7.

4. J. H. Sheridan. A Star in the GM Heavens. *Industry Week*, March 18, 1991, 22-26.

5. R. Henkoff. Cost Cutting: How to Do It Right. *Fortune*, April 9, 1990, 40-49.

6. R. Henkoff. Cost Cutting: How to Do It Right. *Fortune*, April 9, 1990, 40-49.

7. R. Henkoff. Cost Cutting: How to Do It Right. *Fortune*, April 9, 1990, 40-49.

8. J. R. Hackman & G. Oldham, *Work Redesign*. Reading: Addison Wesley Publishing Company, 1980.

9. J. Hoerr. The Payoff From Teamwork. *Business Week*, July 10, 1989, 56-62.

10. B. Dumaine. Who Needs A Boss? *Fortune*, May 7, 1990, 52-60.

11. R. Henkoff. Cost Cutting: How to Do It Right. *Fortune*, April 9, 1990, 40-49.

12. This survey was adapted from the original questionnaire developed and used at Yale University by Hackman and Oldham. For a more comprehensive coverage of the concepts, instruments, and the *Motivating Potential Score* see: J. R. Hackman & G. Oldham, *Work Redesign*. Reading: Addison Wesley Publishing Company, 1980.

Chapter

3 THREE

Developing Teams

"Good organizations are living bodies that grow new muscles to meet challenges. [An organization] chart demoralizes people. Nobody thinks of himself as below other people. And in a good company, he isn't."
    —Robert Townsend
      former President, Avis-Rent-a-Car, Inc.

"He who would learn to fly one day must first learn to stand and walk and run and climb and dance; one cannot fly into flying."
    —Friederich Nietzsche
      German Philosopher

Human resource development professionals are fueling the transition of corporate America to team-based organizations with studies of the team development process.

In the past decade, studies of how teams develop and grow define many different models documenting the trek to becoming truly effective. As you will see, most of these models are amazingly similar since they all describe a very similar team developmental progression:

• *Forming* — Cautious affiliation to the team
• *Storming* — Competitive team relationships
• *Norming* — Harmonious cohesiveness among team members
• *Performing* — Collaborative teamwork

The implication is that all groups must develop through this predetermined sequence if they are to mature into fully effective teams. The further implication is that the forces at work dictate that teams and their members go through a sometimes prolonged, and often painful, trial-and-error process as teams attempt to achieve their task objectives while working through the inevitable relationship issues that naturally arise when people work together.

This chapter presents research on the developmental stages through which teams progress — or stall — when left to their own devices. It's argued that this type of trial-and-error, hit-or-miss approach is much too wasteful of time, effort, and output.

We'll discuss a behavioral teamwork model and developmental process tied to teamwork skills, which helps short-circuit the inefficient, unproductive, and relationship-straining stages of natural development — and enables teams to achieve a collaborative teamwork pattern more quickly.

Developmental Stages of Teams

It appears that teams develop according to an inherent plan, moving through a series of fairly predictable growth stages. Exhibit 3-1 summarizes the strikingly similar phases of team development identified by a variety of researchers.

Source	Stage 1	Stage 2	Stage 3	Stage 4
D. Francis and D. Young[1]	Testing	Infighting	Getting Organized	Mature Closeness
J.E. Jones and W.L. Bearley[2]	Immature Group	Fractionated Group	Sharing Group	Effective Team
J. Moosbruker[3]	Orientation to Group and Task	Conflict over Control	Group Formation and Solidarity	Differentiation and Productivity
S.D. Orsburn, L. Moran, E. Musselwhite and J. Zenger[4]	State of Confusion	Leader Centered	Tightly Formed	Self-Directed
B.W. Tuckman[5]	Forming	Storming	Norming	Performing
G.H. Varney[6]	Formation	Building	Working	Maturity
M. Woodcock and D. Francis[7]	Ritual Sniffing	Infighting	Experimentation	Effectiveness and Maturity

Exhibit 3-1: Team Development Models

Research conducted at Psychological Associates' Consulting Group casts doubts on the validity of some of the developmental dynamics suggested by these models, but here are the details on the four stages.

Developmental Stage 1 — Forming
(Cautious Affiliation to the Team)

As the descriptions in Exhibit 3-1 suggest, Stage 1 is an exploration period, laden with questions but short on answers. In this early stage, members' attachment to the team is tentative. In fact, some members may even lobby behind the scenes — with their bosses, with the team leader — to be excused from participation.

Even those who want to stay are cautious and guarded. Most are anxious about what the team and they, as individual members, are supposed to do. They're concerned about their collective and individual ability to accomplish the tasks ahead, whatever those tasks might turn out to be.

Studying the designated team leader and others in the group, team members assess others' abilities and attitudes, trying to determine how and where they fit into the group. As they explore the boundaries of acceptable individual and team behavior, searching for norms and roles, they're generally vigilant for early signs of group problems; and they're worried about the team's ability to cope with conflict.

Little is accomplished during Stage 1. Productivity is low; and working relationships are guarded, cautious, and noncommittal.

Stage 2 — Storming
(Competitive and Strained Relationships)

Members seem to feel "time's a wastin'" as they first grow impatient with the team's lack of progress, then become overly zealous. Finally getting down to business, they realize that the team's job is different and more difficult that they initially imagined. This discrepancy between initial hopes and expectations and the reality of the situation leads to frustration and anger. Some even resist team goals and tasks as they now appear to be defined. Others question the wisdom of those who started the project in the first place and assigned members to the team.

Consequently, there is much blaming, defensiveness, destructive disagreement, and testy confrontation — especially with the team leader or those vying for a dominant position. Subgroups may form and polarize, with the factions infighting and competing for influence — arguing even when they agree on essential issues.

At this stage, individual members are relying solely on their previous individual experiences, both personal and professional. Most are unaware — or perhaps simply unappreciative — of the unique and valuable talents of other group members. There's resistance to collaboration with other team members — except, perhaps, as allies aligned against an opposing faction.

Hitting the issues of mission, goals, roles, and working agreements head on — and hitting them feverishly — the group makes some progress toward accomplishing its task. However, working relationships take a beating. Although members are learning more about one another, they're typically experiencing team members' worst sides.

Stage 3 — Norming
(Harmonious Cohesiveness Among Members)
"We're in this together, like it or not," might be the dominant attitude as Stage 3 begins. But by the end of this stage, members have discovered that they, in fact, "like it." They like the team as an entity, the members as individuals, their increasingly social encounters, and the sense of belonging.

With the urgent Stage 2 questions of mission, goals, tasks, roles, and standards at least partially resolved, members become less dissatisfied. Predictably, there's significantly decreased animosity toward the leader and other team members. Previously warring factions mellow into normal, healthy, interpersonal patterns.

As a result of their ongoing contact, members have finally begun to understand each other, accept others' individuality, and respect the different abilities of other members. Previously competitive relationships become cooperative, close, and mutually supportive. As communication channels open and feelings of mutual trust deepen, members may even confide in each other as friends, sharing personal problems. During this developmental stage, individuals discover that they're proud to be associated with the team.

Celebrating this newfound "we-ness," the team shifts its focus from its work to maintaining good working order, protecting camaraderie, and avoiding any conflict that might endanger the team's treasured cohesiveness. The emphasis is on harmony and conformity.

As positive feelings among members grow and self-esteem flourishes, team effort is reinforced. As individual and communal skills develop, there are slow increases in the quantity and quality of work. In general, though, the zeal for tangible results which characterized Stage 2 is lost, as members bask in the honeymoon-like happiness of their new, harmonious team relationships.

Stage 4 — Performing (Collaborative Teamwork)

By now, there's general agreement among the members about who they are, what they're doing, and where they're going. During Stage 2, they began to clarify performance expectations and organize to accomplish team goals. During Stage 3, they strengthened interpersonal relationships. Now, during Stage 4, the group jells as a truly collaborative team.

Structured processes and procedures emerge to coordinate resources, communicate openly, resolve interpersonal conflict, and deal with the larger organization. Now that members possess some insight into individual and group processes and behavior, they begin to define high standards for evaluating team and individual performance.

The team makes decisions about task and process, diagnosing and solving (or anticipating and preventing) problems, and choosing and implementing actions and changes. And, in the process, team members communicate candidly and constructively, without fear of rejection. Viewpoints and information are freely shared and pooled to make sound decisions. Constructive conflict is welcomed as a springboard to more creative problem solutions.

Leadership is now participative and involving, with members neither deferring to the designated leader (as happened in Stage 1) nor resisting (the tendency in Stage 2). During Stage 4, the team acts autonomously, sharing power among the membership. Team members are motivated by pride in their accomplishments and a sense of ownership and belonging. Individual and coordinated task expertise leads to peak performance levels.

The Real World of Teamwork

Occasionally, through a prolonged and painful process of trial and error, a team eventually evolves to the productive and efficient state of affairs described in Stage 4. The question that arises is how to shortcut this process.

The validity of the team development stages is well established in observations of real-world teams. Disruptive, ineffective, and unproductive team behavior is easily classified as *Forming*, *Storming*, and *Norming*, and a high-performance team displays *Performing* behaviors a good deal of the time. A sample of the behaviors classified by development stage appears in Exhibit 3-2.

Exhibit 3-2 Behavior Classification

Stage 1
Forming

- Pride in being chosen but anticipation about what lies ahead
- Impersonal, watchful, guarded, cautious behavior
- Tentative attachment to the team
- Members cautiously exploring boundaries of acceptable individual and team behavior
- Tendency to avoid others — be "loners"
- Little real communication
- Suspicion, fear, anxiety about the task ahead
- Some anxiety about why they are there, why others are there, who'll lead the group, and what they'll do
- Weak attempts to define the task

Stage 2
Storming

- Impatience with lack of progress
- Focus on team production without regard for the needs of team members
- Domination by one or several team members
- Overly competitive and confrontational
- Self-serving — "Look out for yourself" attitude
- One-way communication
- People becoming testy, blameful, overzealous
- Frustration, anger, and resistance to goals
- Defensiveness, competition, infighting

Stage 3
Norming

- Competitive relationships becoming cooperative
- Relief in believing that team issues will be worked out
- Team relationships emphasized even at expense of productivity
- Sense of team cohesion and close attachment to the team
- Team showing strong concern for the needs of team members
- Agreements, norms, procedures for working together
- Communication that is open in all directions, active, and candid
- Feelings of mutual trust, respect, and harmony
- Team focus on building harmony and managing conflict

Stage 4
Performing

- High productivity as a result of working collaboratively toward common goals
- Clear mission, goals, roles, and performance expectations
- Agreement on who they are, what they are doing, and where they are going
- Involvement of all team members in achieving important tasks
- Cooperative and productive team climate
- Open, relevant, business-like communication
- Ability to prevent or work through tough team issues
- Insights into group processes
- Understanding of others' strengths and weaknesses

However, the described, linear process of team development — that all teams progress orderly and systematically through the four stages — runs counter to our experience and research with teams. We find that many so-called teams in the real world never achieve optimal performance. Some stall and lose their way. Others regress to an earlier stage. Some groups that call themselves teams are little more than loose collections of individuals with nothing more in common than their names on a team roster and a few common meetings.

In-name-only teams abound in corporate America. We made this discovery in a multi-year study of teamwork patterns displayed by teams at all levels in Fortune 500 companies.

Our research began with a behavioral model of teamwork patterns adapted from the Dimensional Model of Leadership developed years earlier by Lefton and his colleagues at Psychological Associates.[8]

The model, consisting of two dimensions — *Getting Things Done* and *Building Strong Relationships* — reflects the two common categories of task- and people-related behaviors displayed by teams.

Ideally, teams develop missions, set goals, organize roles, and structure their activities to *get things done.* Teams *build strong relationships* by promoting open communication, sharing resources, and coordinating — and by fostering active participation — while they're making decisions, solving problems, conducting meetings, or managing conflicts.

This model, shown in Exhibit 3-3, further defines four distinct patterns of teamwork, which correspond to the stages of team development: Stage 1 — *Forming*; Stage 2 — *Storming*; Stage 3 — *Norming*; and Stage 4 — *Performing*.

Next we developed descriptions of common team functions — such as setting goals, communicating, appraising performance, managing conflict — that corresponded to the four behavioral patterns. Using these descriptions, we were able to place teams under a social microscope and determine the amount of each pattern displayed as each team function is performed.

Team members evaluated seven team functions. They allocated 100 points reflecting the extent (percent of time) that each of the four patterns characterized the team. Point allotments were supported by specific behavior examples. After reviewing the individual assessments, the team discussed and reached a numerical consensus on how the team operated on each of the seven team functions — how much *Forming, Storming, Norming,* and *Performing* behavior typically characterized team functioning.

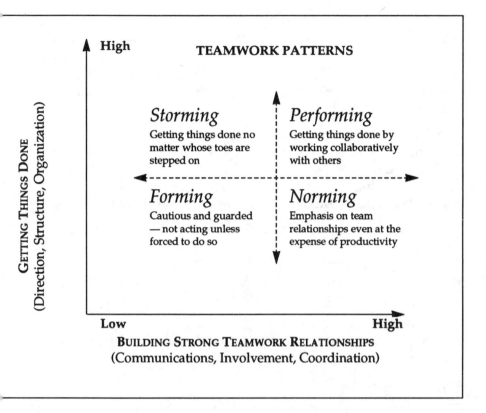

GETTING THINGS DONE
(Direction, Structure, Organization)

High

TEAMWORK PATTERNS

Storming

Getting things done no
matter whose toes are
stepped on

Performing

Getting things done by
working collaboratively
with others

Forming

Cautious and guarded
— not acting unless
forced to do so

Norming

Emphasis on team
relationships even at the
expense of productivity

Low   High

BUILDING STRONG TEAMWORK RELATIONSHIPS
(Communications, Involvement, Coordination)

Exhibit 3-3: Dimensional Model of Teamwork Patterns

Seventy-one teams described only 36% of their behavior as
typifying Stage 4 — *Performing.*

Roughly 24% of the behavior displayed by the teams was
characteristic of Stage 1 — *Forming.* One respondent described the
lack of involvement typical of Stage 1 teams this way: "How can
there be conflicts when we're all busy keeping our distance from
one another? We just don't interact enough to generate conflict."

Stage 1 teams tend to go through the motions, all the while
maintaining the status quo. As one participant reported: "Our
meetings give new meaning to the word 'dull.' The boss makes a
few pronouncements; then the rest of us make a few
announcements; then we adjourn. Usually, it could be done just as
well by memo."

Nearly a third (30%) of the team behavior described by survey participants was entrenched in Stage 2 — *Storming*; and some teams seemed unlikely to move past it. One participant explained: "Our problem is we don't want to resolve our conflicts. We enjoy them too much. We thrive on them. It may be counterproductive, but conflict's a way of life with us."

Implicit in most of the Stage 2 behavior was the fact that the struggle for dominance (assuming there had been one) was clearly settled. A team member participating in the survey said: "With us, decision making is a one-man show. The boss makes the decisions, period. We endorse them. It's a very neat division of labor."

The remaining team behavior described by survey participants (10%) was clearly Stage 3 — *Norming*, typified by this response: "It's been years since I last attended a brisk, business-like meeting. When we meet, we spin our heels on small talk, war stories, and inside gossip. It's fun — but what do we accomplish?"

Left to its own devices, without guidance or direction, a naturally evolving team would zig zag back and fourth among the four quadrants before ever reaching Stage 4.

This is illustrated in Exhibit 3-4.

Challenged by the practical implications of this discovery, it seemed logical to pursue a direct pathway to optimal team performance. The resulting plan for quick, but complete, team development is illustrated in Exhibit 3-5.

This direct pathway to a *Performing* team respects the natural evolutionary inclination of most teams by first addressing issues related to task accomplishment — setting overall mission and direction, formulating challenging goals, defining clear roles, and developing standards and a team appraisal process. But here's the critical difference between free-form team development and the guided developmental process mapped out in Exhibit 3-5: *While addressing task-oriented concerns, teams simultaneously develop open communication, active participation, supportive sharing of resources, and ongoing review and feedback.*

When team members get things done *while* building strong relationships, they merge purely task-oriented lessons of Stage 2 with the purely relationship-oriented lessons of Stage 3 — and consequently reach Stage 4 more quickly. In fact, everything a

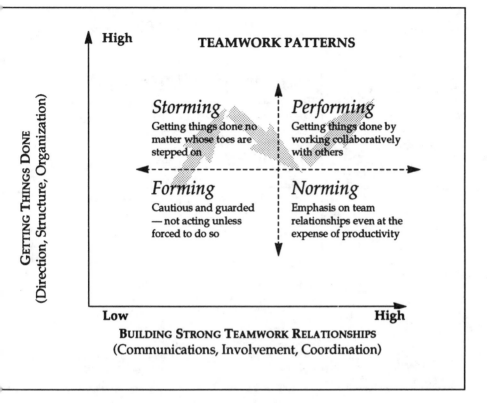

Exhibit 3-4: Dimensional Model of Teamwork Patterns

team does must be directed simultaneously at the twin goals of getting things done (task accomplishment) *and* building strong teamwork (encouraging active participation, open communication, and supportive relationships).

A Micro View of Teamwork Patterns and Team Dynamics

The question remains: What happens after a team reaches Stage 4? Or, does a team ever fully develop to Stage 4, displaying True Teamwork patterns in every aspect of team functioning?

While the literature on the stages of team development suggests that teams naturally evolve and fully develop into a Stage 4 collaborative team, our research proves otherwise. Using the teamwork model and assessment process described earlier, we were able to measure team development on important operations such as decision making, goal setting, meetings, communication, and resolving conflict.

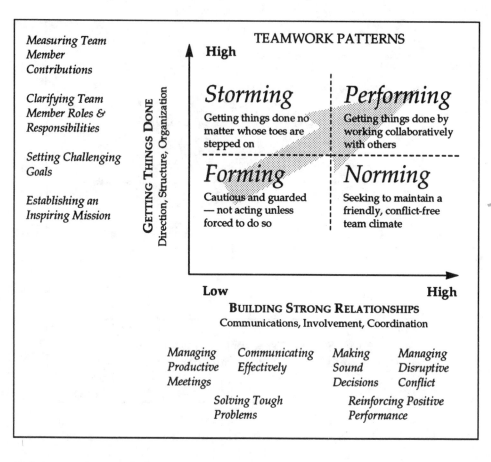

Exhibit 3-5: Direct Pathway to True Teamwork

Exhibit 3-6 illustrates how a sample of 71 Fortune 500 teams described their teamwork patterns on seven important team operations.[9]

The percentages indicate consensus among team members on the behavior the team normally displays when engaged in the various team operations.

Based on Tuckman's concept of team development, one would predict that most of the teams' behavior would be assigned to one quadrant reflecting the team's developmental stage. As shown in Exhibit 3-6, though, there's tremendous variability of team behavior across all stages and all functions — whether you're looking at a single team or the aggregate shown in the exhibit.

	Internal Coordination	Team Communications	Managing Conflict	Team Meetings	Team Decision Making	Team Goal Setting	Appraisal and Feedback
Stage 1 *Form*	24%	25%	26%	24%	23%	16%	25%
Stage 2 *Storm*	38%	31%	31%	26%	29%	29%	25%
Stage 3 *Norm*	7%	12%	11%	13%	9%	9%	15%
Stage 4 *Perform*	31%	32%	32%	37%	39%	46%	35%

xhibit 3-6: Assessment of Teamwork Patterns for 71 Teams

Teams invariably show vestiges of each stage and the patterns vary from function to function.

As seen in Exhibit 3-6, the most well-developed team operation is goal setting — a rather mechanical function and relatively unemotional topic for most teams. Look at communication, conflict management, and coordination and you see significantly less Stage 4. These patterns of Stage 4 behavior suggest that the more emotionally laden the function, the more difficult it is to develop teamwork into a Stage 4, fully functioning team.

This data makes it clear that teams do *not* move predictably through the developmental stages. Rather, teams display a mixture of behavior that varies by function. By pigeonholing a team into a specific teamwork stage, the complexity of team behavior is treated quite simplistically.

Our data also suggests that team development is not a one-shot proposition — it must be ongoing. Stage 4 — *Performing* teamwork should be defined in clear behavioral standards for the team, and an ongoing process of diagnosis, critique, and appraisal must be used — supplemented by proper training — to build on strengths (increase Stage 4 behavior) and shore up weak spots (decrease Stages 1, 2, and 3 behavior).

Getting things done (focusing on direction, organization, and structure) and building relationships (getting active involvement, communication, and coordination) must be developed simultaneously in each team operation. Only then will a team approximate and sustain the behaviors we define as the Stage 4 teamwork pattern.

Conclusion

Teams and team members, when left to their own devices — primarily trial-and-error experimentation — do tend to mirror the sequential four-stage process described in the literature. However, teams do not follow a consistent developmental pattern like that of a genetically programmed caterpillar-to-butterfly sequence. Teams, at any given point in time, are most apt to demonstrate a mixture of the characteristics within the four stages.

In other words, it is unlikely that a team will ever be a "pure" type (*Forming, Storming, Norming,* or *Performing*). The reason why teams, whether early or late in formation, tend to be a mixture is that their behavior and effectiveness are functions of how they structure themselves to accomplish the specific business task they are charged with — and how effectively their relationships promote open communication and collaboration.

On most teams, direction, structure, organization skills, and relationship-building skills are apt to be unequally developed or unevenly applied in any given team activity. For example, a team with clear team direction and purpose may lack definition of roles and responsibilities. A team may be effective at getting involvement and accomplishing results in meetings, but team decision-making activities may be laden with destructive conflict and disagreement. A team may have clear standards of performance, but the manner in which they were imposed on the team may result in low commitment to adhering to them.

Inefficient trial-and-error team development must be replaced with specific diagnosis and early identification of the structural and relationship needs of the team. Then, and only then, can training be targeted to the needs of teams and the specific developmental objectives they have. One-shot training, however, is not the answer. Teams and their needs will change and develop over time. Unproductive and relationship-damaging behavior that has been dealt with effectively in the past will likely reappear.

Development of teamwork and the skills associated with it must, therefore, be considered an ongoing process.

Endnotes

1. D. Francis & D. Young. *Improving Work Groups: A Practical Manual for Team Building*. San Diego: University Associates, Inc., 1979.

2. J. E. Jones & W. L. Bearley. *Group Development Assessment*. Bryn Mawr: Organization Design and Development, 1986.

3. J. Mossbruker. Developing a Productivity Team: Making Groups and Work Teams Work. In W. B. Reddy & K. Jamison (Eds.) *Team Building: Blueprints for Productivity and Satisfaction*. Co-published by NTL Institute for Applied Behavioral Sciences and University Associates, Inc., 1988.

4. S. D. Orsburn, L. Moran, E. Musselwhite & J. Zenger. *Self-Directed Work Teams: The New American Challenge*. Homewood: Business One Irwin, 1990.

5. B. W. Tuckman. Developmental Sequence in Small Groups. *Psychological Bulletin*, (63), 384-389, 1965.

6. G. H. Varney. *Building Productive Teams: An Action Guide and Resource Book*. San Francisco: Jossey-Bass, 1991.

7. M. Woodcock & D. Francis. Team Building: Yes or No. In W. W. Burke and L. D. Goodstein (Eds.) *Trends and Issues in OD: Current Theory and Practice*. San Diego: University Associates, 1980.

8. R. E. Lefton, V. R. Buzzotta & M. Sherberg. *Improving Productivity Through People Skills* (Chapter 18 — Teams and Teamwork). Cambridge: Ballinger Publishing Co., 1980.

9. Based on unpublished norms from Psychological Associates' Consulting Group's Dimensional Team Building seminars.

Chapter

4 OUR

Building Team Structure and Skills

*"It's not just a question of people feeling good
about each other and the company. A completely
diverse group must agree on a goal, put the notion
of individual accountability aside and figure out
how to work with each other. Most of all, they must
learn that if the team fails, it's everyone's fault."*
　　—*Douglas K. Smith*
　　　Co-Author, Wisdom of Teams

Y ou're a member of a team — whether you realize it or not, whether your "team" is called a team or not. You have to work with other people to get your job done.

You may sometimes work alone. But you can't work in total isolation. Deliver your work on time and done correctly, and team results improve. Work slowly or finish late — make mistakes — and everyone on the team pays the price.

In this chapter you'll assess your teamwork on the macro level — team patterns that typify your team. Then you'll do a micro-level assessment of team strengths and improvement areas in terms of direction, structure, and team skills. This will help identify opportunities to achieve synergistic teamwork.

Synergistic Teamwork

In theory, by collaborating in pursuit of a common goal, team members will synergize — that is, produce results more valuable than the mere sum of their individual contributions. Ideally, then, teamwork is multiplicative, not simply additive of individual member contributions.

Syn • er • gy ('sin-ər-je) noun.
• When the team gets a result that can't be achieved by any one person.
• When the team result is better than the sum of individual contributions.
• When people work exceptionally well together.

In practice, though, many teams never synergize. Other teams do so less than they might. At worse, teamwork is not only not multiplicative, it's subtractive — the members would have been better off working separately.

When teams have clear direction, structure, and organization and team skills to communicate and collaborate effectively, it is generally agreed that: **Working as a team is** *more productive* **and** *more fun than working alone.*

Common Best and Worst Team Experiences

Exhibit 4-1 shows some of the common behaviors that support or get in the way of synergistic teamwork. How many have you observed?

Team Leader / Team Member Behavior

The behaviors of the team leader or member can help or hinder teamwork. You have a choice — Form, Storm, Norm, or Perform. The choice is yours. Exhibit 4-2 shows team leader and member behaviors that can help or hinder teamwork.

Assessing Your Patterns

Read the descriptions of the four teamwork patterns on page 55. Allocate 100 points among the statements to reflect the percentage of each pattern that is characteristic of how your team typically operates. You can allocate points to some or all of the four patterns. However, the total of points you give to all four patterns must equal 100. Explain your allocations with specific examples of team behavior.

Best Team Experiences	Worst Team Experiences
• People arrive fully prepared. • Mission and goals are clear. • People talk openly and listen intently to one another. • All members freely share resources. • People work out their disagreements. • Team members remain open-minded to new ideas. • Meetings end with clear decisions and actions.	• People arrive to meetings unprepared. • Goals are unclear. • People interrupt and do more talking than listening. • Some members do their "own thing." • There is a lot of arguing and fighting. • People are stubborn and closed-minded to new ideas. • Meetings end without decisions or actions.

Exhibit 4-1: Best and Worst Team Experiences

Teamwork Pattern	Team Leader Behavior	Team Member Behavior
Forming "Don't rock the boat." "Avoid getting too involved."	• Puts off making decisions and taking action • Resists change • Gives little information	• Talks and listens little • Avoids getting involved • Does just enough to get by • Cautious and guarded
Storming "I say and you do." "What can you do for me?"	• Pushes own agenda • Squelches disagreement • Punishes mistakes • Doesn't ask for opinions	• Talks more than listens • Argues • Sticks to own position • Blames, finds fault, puts others down
Norming "Let's build friendly team relationships." "Let's be friends."	• Establishes rules and boundaries • Tries to build morale and team support • Very positive and upbeat	• Confides in others • Is friendly and supportive • Builds one-for-all and all-for-one climate
Performing "Let's work together to achieve team results." "We can achieve the best results through teamwork."	• Helps the team decide what it will achieve • Keeps people informed and involved • Lets people know how they're doing	• Freely shares information and resources • Probes others' ideas • Uses conflict as a springboard to greater creativity

Exhibit 4-2: Team Leader and Team Member Behaviors

Teamwork Pattern	Your Points	Explanation
Forming: We don't accomplish much as a team. We prefer keeping distance and working with one another only as necessary. If pressured, we do sometimes work together, but there's little mutual support and coordination and a lot of cautious, guarded behavior.		
Storming: We tend not to work well as a team. When we do work together, there is a lot of arguing, destructive conflict, and hostility. Most of our interactions are self-serving and designed to bolster our own positions and put the views and ideas of others down.		
Norming: We try to get along well together. We work through problems and disagreements that interfere with team cohesiveness. We spend much of our time managing group process and, as a result, business and task issues are neglected.		
Performing: We set clear goals and ensure everyone knows what's expected. We are truly synergistic — we have strong coordination, open communication, and mutual support. Everyone is involved, helping the team achieve its task and improving team relationships.		

TOTAL: 100

Number of Performing Points

Write the number of *Performing* points you gave your team in the Performing quadrant below.

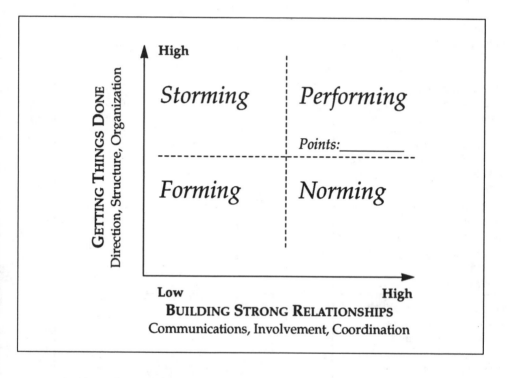

Performing Points
- 9 - 8 Excellent Team Direction, Organization, and Skills
- 7 - 6 Some Fine-Tuning Needed
- 5 - 1 Improvement Required in Several Areas

Strengths	Improvement Areas

Developmental Planning

In Chapter 3, we discussed team development.

Teams must address *Getting Things Done* — providing direction, structure, and organization — to accomplish important tasks and projects.

Teams also must address *Building Strong Working Relationships* — skills needed to promote open communications, involvement, and coordination in important team activities like meetings, problem solving, decision making, and conflict resolution.

By providing clear direction, organization, and structure and building team skills for open communication, involvement, and coordination, you'll help accelerate team development along a direct pathway as shown in Exhibit 4-3.

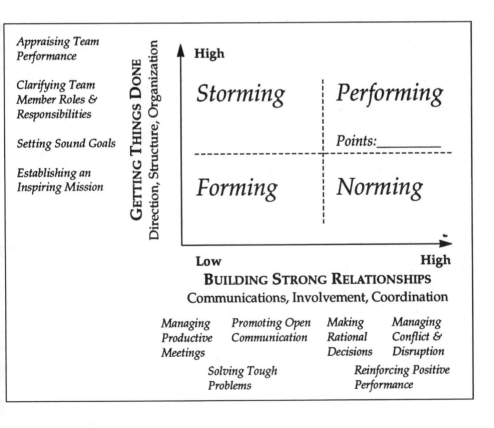

Exhibit 4-3: Direct Pathway to Team Development

Committing to Continuous Team Improvement

What you do to develop your team will depend on how effectively you are currently operating and the barriers getting in the way of your functioning even better. The important thing is to commit to continuous team improvement. That's what you'll begin doing now. You'll circle the number that reflects your agreement with each statement in Parts 1 and 2. This helps diagnose team strengths and areas needing further development.

PART 1 Direction, Structure & Organization	Disagree Strongly	Disagree	Disagree Slightly	Agree Slightly	Agree	Agree Strongly
1. We have a clear and exciting mission describing our purpose, our customers, our commitment to quality and service, and how we'll work as a team.	0	1	2	3	4	5
2. We have challenging team goals with specific performance targets and detailed action steps to guide us toward important job objectives.	0	1	2	3	4	5
3. Each person understands his/her team role, authority for making decisions and taking action, and how he/she must support others on the team.	0	1	2	3	4	5
4. We have clear procedures for meetings, problem solving and decision making, and for working with other units that keep us focused on our goals.	0	1	2	3	4	5
5. We have systems for regularly reviewing our performance and identifying actions for improving team results and the contribution of each member.	0	1	2	3	4	5

PART 2 Team Skills & Practices	Disagree Strongly	Disagree	Disagree Slightly	Agree Slightly	Agree	Agree Strongly
1. We meet only when there's good reason and our meetings are to the point, involve all team members, and end with clear action plans.	0	1	2	3	4	5
2. We have problem-solving and decision-making methods that help us generate quality decisions and solutions to which people feel committed.	0	1	2	3	4	5
3. Team members communicate openly and effectively, listen to one another's views, and have productive discussions about important job issues.	0	1	2	3	4	5
4. We are skilled at dealing with personal conflicts among team members before things get disruptive and out of hand.	0	1	2	3	4	5
5. We have systems for regularly reviewing our performance and identifying actions for improving team results and the contribution of each member.	0	1	2	3	4	5

Scoring the Survey

You'll average and chart your team scores on the survey. This will help you determine where to begin improving teamwork and enhancing productivity.

Circle the range that contains your team average on all items in the column labeled "Part 1." Do the same for "Part 2." Review the description of the level of functioning and developmental need associated with each score. This will illustrate your overall need for development.

PART 1 Direction, Structure & Organization	Description	PART 2 Team Skills & Practices
22 - 25	Fully Functioning Team — No need for development	22 - 25
18 - 21	Functioning Team — Few needs for development	18 - 21
14 - 17	Functioning Team — Several needs for development	14 - 17
10 - 13	Many aspects of Team functioning need development	10 - 13
less than 10	Nearly all aspects of Team functioning need development	less than 10

Now plot your team average *item* scores for Parts 1 and 2 below:

PART 1: Direction, Structure & Organization

Scores less than 3 need immediate attention	Developmental Priority
Item 1: 0 1 2 3 4 5	• Establishing an Inspiring Mission
Item 2: 0 1 2 3 4 5	• Setting Sound Goals
Item 3: 0 1 2 3 4 5	• Clarifying Roles, Responsibilities, Authorities
Item 4: 0 1 2 3 4 5	• Establishing Working Procedures
Item 5: 0 1 2 3 4 5	• Appraising Team Performance

PART 2: Team Skills & Practices

Scores less than 3 need immediate attention	Developmental Priority
Item 1: 0 1 2 3 4 5	• Managing Productive Meetings
Item 2: 0 1 2 3 4 5	• Sound Problem Solving & Decision Making
Item 3: 0 1 2 3 4 5	• Promoting Open Communication
Item 4: 0 1 2 3 4 5	• Managing Conflict & Disruption
Item 5: 0 1 2 3 4 5	• Coordination on the Team & with Other Units

Building on Strengths and Addressing Development Needs

The remainder of this book provides practical tips and proven techniques for building on strengths and addressing development needs. Each chapter focuses on a particular issue which, if addressed, will help improve team direction, organization, structure, and teamwork.

The chapters are organized similarly. Each begins with an introduction to the topic followed by a Road Map. This Road Map allows you to go right to the section that addresses the most immediate need of the team. You can review the tips and techniques as you need them and immediately apply them with the team back on the job. Doing so will help accelerate the development of teamwork and make your team interactions both fun and productive.

Bear in mind that teamwork is a continuous process — it must be continuously developed through team self-appraisal, feedback, and developmental planning. If the process is continuous, you'll build a high-performance team that gets results while strengthening working relationships. That's a pretty tall order — but if you and your team members are willing to invest the time and attention needed, your effort will pay handsome dividends for all involved.

Chapter

5IVE

Establishing an Inspiring Mission

"If you don't know where you're going,
any road will get you there."
        —Alice in Wonderland

"The very essence of leadership is [that] you
have to have a vision. It's got to be a vision you
articulate clearly and forcefully on every occasion.
You can't blow an uncertain trumpet."
        —Father Theodore Hesburgh
            former President, Notre Dame

"It must come out loud and clear in the advertising campaign that we're the best value in the industry," Terry asserted. "I disagree totally," quipped Anne. "I think it's time we let people know how convenient it is to do business with us." The meeting was nearly three hours old and the members were nowhere near a resolution.

Bob remained silent through the lively exchange. His thoughts were on the mission the team finalized not more than two weeks earlier. "Let's remind ourselves of our mission," he stated.

As he recited the heavily debated phrase, the room remained silent: "Our mission is to guarantee total satisfaction to our customers — that's what we agreed will differentiate us from our competition. If we believe this, we should be bold enough to go public with it as a way of asking people to hold us accountable." Silence continued as if the team was ashamed at having overlooked the obvious.

Effective teamwork requires first and foremost an inspiring mission — a general statement of team purpose and direction that members rally behind and use as a guiding and motivating statement of what ideally they can become. Mission must come before strategy, goals, plans, and actions.[1] Whether teamwork occurs in the context of an orchestra, football team, military unit, departmental or project team, one principal is universal: teamwork requires commitment to an exciting and lucid vision of a preferred future.

A mission provides a sense of purpose for teamwork. Motivation is enhanced since people see themselves as an important part of a worthwhile endeavor. As a result, team members are more likely to bring vigor and enthusiasm to the task.

In addition, a mission provides the basis for developing goals, plans, and tactics that bridge the present to a preferred future. It helps clarify roles, responsibilities, and coordination requirements so members know exactly why they're there, what they'll contribute, and how they'll work together as a team.

Finally, a mission provides the basis for making decisions, solving problems, and managing in a way that constantly advances the current situation toward a desired future.

This chapter is about team mission. It will help you define and build commitment to a clear and exciting future. It will guide you in continually enhancing your mission and using it as a blueprint for fully realizing the potential of teamwork.

Road Map

Definitions — Missions and Visions

The distinction between missions and visions, if there is one, has not been fully clarified in the management literature. When in doubt, go to the dictionary. Webster differentiates the terms as follows:

- Mission — a task or function assigned or undertaken.
- Vision — the act or power of imagination.

Warren Bennis and Burt Nanus, writing in *Leaders*, state:[2]

To choose a direction, a leader must first have developed a mental image of a possible and desirable future state of the organization. This image, which we call a vision, may be as vague as a dream or as precise as a goal or mission statement. The critical point is that a vision articulates a view of a realistic, credible, attractive future for the organization, a condition that is better in some important ways than what now exists. A vision is a target that beckons (p. 89).

Tom Peters describes eight criteria of effective missions. The mission must be:[3]

1. Inspirational — providing an uplifting idea about what the team can ideally become.
2. Clear and challenging — describing a clear future state, not simply a description of the current situation.
3. Differentiating — describing the "uniqueness" and how the organization can position itself as being distinctly different from the competition.
4. Stable but constantly challenged — providing direction and stability over time, adjusting as required to account for changes in surroundings.
5. Beacons and controls — providing the understanding of basic values and direction so people can live it with unswerving consistency.
6. Empowering — helping to draw forth the best from people.
7. Future-oriented — renewing basic values and commitments while giving people the confidence to embark on a bold new direction.
8. Lived in details, not broad strokes — focusing the day-to-day actions and setting the current situation in motion toward a preferred future.

In *Managing for Excellence,* David Bradford and Allan Cohen argue that establishing an operative vision requires two very different tasks:[4]

Establishing an operative overarching goal (i.e., a vision) requires two distinctly different tasks of the leader: to formulate an appropriate overarching goal and to gain its acceptance by the members. Each task requires different sets of skills. The first task demands intuitive and analytical ability to sense what would excite subordinates, even though they themselves might not be able to; the second requires inspirational and selling ability. Common to both sets of skills is an ability to think beyond the daily routine, to see a greater vision that ties day-to-day activities to significant future goals (p. 112).

In this chapter we'll use the terms vision and mission to:
• Assert what the team can be at its best, or
• Point people toward a solution to a problem, or
• Define superordinate or overarching goals for the team.

We'll assume that a mission is a thorough and more complete charter defining what business or businesses the team is in, what services/products are to be offered to which customers, and team values about customer service, product quality, and how the team will work together.

We'll assume that a vision is more like a motto. It's easy to remember — it's a more concise and plaque-like statement that serves the team as a reminder of its mission and can be communicated to customers and others as a way of asking them to hold the team accountable. The vision is developed only after a detailed mission is thoroughly crafted by the team.

We'll provide more structure and definition to mission and vision later. But first, let's look at some examples.

At Avis, "We're #2, We Try Harder." This slogan or vision was part of the advertising campaign of Avis for years. More important, it was part of a well-conceived plan for the corporation. Hertz clearly was the number one company in the car rental business and Avis was realistic enough to acknowledge it.

The differentiation Avis wanted in order to maintain market share was service — *we try harder to achieve customer satisfaction* was the message. Content being number two in the rental business, Avis aspired to be number one in sales of used cars. Its strategy was to maintain careful records of maintenance and take cars out of service at about 30 thousand miles. Doing so allowed the company to offer the public a carefully maintained, low mileage, used car. And sales of used cars flourished.

Here's another example. Stew Leonard, a grocer in Norwalk, Connecticut, has only one store but sales are in excess of $90 million. Stew codifies the company's uniqueness in one simple statement: "Rule Number 1: The customer is always right. Rule Number 2: If the customer is wrong, see Rule Number 1."

To reinforce this value, Stew had a three-ton stone placed conspicuously at the store's entrance with the two rules engraved in bold letters. One day a newly hired clerk was confronted by a disgruntled shopper who had lost her engraved Parker pen that she had received as a gift. She thought she lost it in the store and stopped at the lost-and-found department. The clerk could not find the pen but, seeing the woman's visible distress, produced several $20 gift certificates. Not surprisingly, the customer went away happy.

Was Stew Leonard upset? Absolutely not. Recognizing the long-term revenue stream from satisfied customers, Stew applauded the clerk and sanctioned the activity in the next company newsletter.

In both examples, the message is clear. Mission and vision embody the company's uniqueness, provide direction for its people, and guide activities like strategy formulation, goal setting, and decision making.

Behavior Model of Team Mission Patterns

The model of team mission patterns consists of two factors — clarity of mission, and involvement and commitment.

Clarity of Mission
An effective team mission clearly identifies and defines:
- The *What* — what the team is organized or exists to do: its purpose or business
- The *Who* — who the team serves: internal and external customers

- The *How* — how the team serves its customers: values about product quality and customer responsiveness; and how the team will work together: values about candor, communication, sharing of resources, mutual support.

xhibit 5-1: Team Mission Elements

The mission must support a higher-level mission or mandate, of which the team is a part. The higher-level mission can be from the department, division, corporation, or other component of the organization.

Involvement and Commitment
Effective team missions are established in a way that involves all team members. When everyone on a team contributes to a mission, team members all share the same understanding and high level of commitment.

The Model of Team Mission Patterns in Exhibit 5-2 shows how a team's mission consists of both clarity and the involvement and commitment of team members that must live it.

Below are examples of each team pattern:
- *Forming*: We don't have a mission, or it's so general and vague it doesn't serve as a unifying force for the team.
- *Storming*: Our team mission is specific and clear but it was mandated — handed to us with little input. As a result, commitment to living it is low.
- *Norming*: We were all actively involved in developing the mission but it contains vague words like "excellent" and "the best." We all agreed to it but our mission provides little direction.
- *Performing*: There's a lot of commitment to our mission, which presents a specific and challenging purpose and an energizing aspiration for the team.

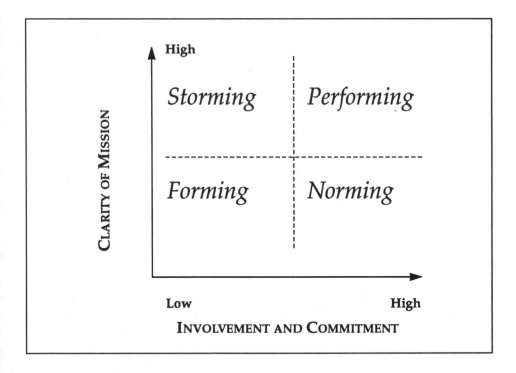

Exhibit 5-2: Model of Team Mission Patterns

Elements of a Mission Statement

A mission can contain many elements but most missions address three core or nuclear elements — Purpose, Customers, and Values.

The What — Purpose of the Team
In defining the purpose of the team, the team specifies what the team is organized to do, the nature of its business, why it exists as a team.

The Who — Customers of the Team
In defining customers, the team specifies who the team serves — internal and external customers, people who will receive and use what the team produces.

The How — Values about Service, Quality, and Teamwork
In defining team values, the team specifies values the team will pursue in serving customers, such as quality, responsiveness, and service, and how team members will work together internally among team members.

Example 1: Space Systems Development Team

Our
Purpose

Our mission is to design rockets that put satellites in precise locations in space. This is essential to support and advance the world's information and communications network.

Our
Customers

Our internal customer is the manufacturing team that must build and deliver functional rockets according to agreed-upon specifications and schedules.

Our external customers are the Government contractors, taxpayers, and ultimately the people who will benefit from satellite communications and information technology.

Our Values
about Service,
Quality, and
Teamwork

We will design systems that are technologically superior to our competitors', adhere to standards established by our manufacturers, and exceed our contractors' expectations for quality, reliability, and safety.

To do so, we must work flawlessly as a team. This means we will avoid narrow functional thinking and individualism.

We will openly communicate, share resources, promote active involvement, and coordinate our efforts as a synergistic unit just as the components of our rockets must operate in flawless synchrony to achieve a successful mission in space.

Example 2: Financial Service Team

Our Purpose	Our mission is to create shareholder wealth, financial security, and peace of mind through a full range of financial planning, investment, and insurance products and services.
Our Customers	Our customers are individuals and their families who reside in rural America who seek investment portfolios with the proper balance of risk and return.
Our Values about Service, Quality, and Teamwork	We will get to know our customers as people, develop strong friendships, educate them to make informed investment decisions, and provide quality products and services that support a conservative investment philosophy. We will keep each other fully informed about new products and services in our areas of specialization and work closely as a team to serve our customers. We will meet at least monthly to answer two questions: "What have we done for our customers since our last meeting?" and "What added value and personalized service can we offer each of our customers in the next 30 days?"

Sample Vision Statements

Earlier we said that a vision is more like a motto. It's a more concise statement that serves the team as a reminder of its mission and can be communicated to customers and others as a way of asking them to hold us accountable.

Oftentimes the vision is the statement appearing on plaques, pocket cards, and the like. While it's shorter than the mission, it delivers the same message.

Some examples of visions are shown in Exhibit 5-3.

Company	Customer	Purpose	Values
Elevator Company	To provide any consumer	a means of moving people and things up, down, and sideways over short distances	with higher reliability than any similar enterprise in the world.
Check Printer	To provide all banks, investment firms, and S&L's	error-free financial instruments delivered in a timely fashion;	error-free means absolutely no errors; timely means a 48-hour turnaround.
Hotel Chain	To provide economy- and quality-minded frequent business travelers	with a premier, moderate-priced lodging facility	which is consistently perceived as clean, comfortable, well maintained, and attractive, staffed by friendly, attentive, efficient people.
Fast Food Restaurant	To offer the fast food customer	food prepared in the same high-quality manner worldwide, tasty and reasonably priced	delivered in a consistent, low-key decor and friendly atmosphere.

Exhibit 5-3: Examples of Visions

A vision is a short statement of the mission. As such, the mission must always precede the vision. The mission captures the full meaning behind the sentences and phases of the vision. Both communicate the what, who, and how.

Getting Involvement and Commitment

A high-quality, clear mission is not a good mission unless there is commitment to living it in the day-to-day actions. Understanding and commitment results from active involvement on the part of all team members in developing the mission. Here are some steps to follow to get team involvement and commitment.

Step 1: Review Mission Elements
Review the elements of a mission — The *What*, *Who*, and *How*.

Step 2: Individual Formulation of the Mission Elements
Each team member should answer the key questions: What is our mission and purpose? Who are our customers? How do we want to go about serving our customers, producing high-quality products, and working together as a team?

Step 3: List Individual Ideas for First Element — Our Purpose
Each team member presents his/her description of the first element and explains it to the team. A recorder will list the ideas. No critique should occur. Ask questions for clarification if needed. Make sure to get each member's ideas up on a flip chart.

Step 4: Team Discussion and Consensus for First Element
Now the team discusses the ideas presented on the flip chart. The discussion should focus on the merits of the various ideas and possible combinations. Team members should keep an open mind, probe others' ideas, and consider the many viewpoints. The discussion should not involve wordsmithing — that will come later. Just discuss the general concepts.

Step 5: Repeat Process
Repeat Steps 3 and 4 for the remaining elements.

Step 6: Task Force Assignment
Assign a task force to forge the team's ideas into a coherent mission. The task force should not change the content or concepts. The task force should polish the words, grammar, and sentence structure.

Step 7: Review of Task Force Draft
The task force presents the draft mission to the team. The team makes any final changes as appropriate to be incorporated into the final mission by the task force.

This task may sound easy but, in reality, it's quite difficult and tests the limits of members' patience. That's because, as Henry Mintzberg points out:[5]

Study after study has shown that managers' . . . activities are typically characterized by brevity, variety, discontinuity, and that [managers] are strongly oriented to action and dislike reflective activities. No study has found important patterns in the way managers schedule their time. They seem to jump from issue to issue, continually responding to the needs of the moment.

Mission statement development is a very reflective activity requiring team members to "muddle through" issues about purpose, direction, and values. Plan on several half-day meetings before the team finalizes its mission. And make sure everyone has a fingerprint or two on the final document.

ommunicating Your Team's Mission

Ensuring that a mission is thorough, high quality, clear, realistic, and specific is still no guarantee that a mission will be effective. Even the best mission may not achieve its objectives unless it's communicated properly.

Your efforts on your team's mission are not finished until you channel its message to everyone in the organization who is affected by it:

- *Management* – If management formed the team, members of the management team will want to know how the team defined its mission.
- *Other teams* – Other teams your team works with may need to know the purpose of your team, objectives you have in common, and how you'll work together.
- *Customers* – Your customers should know the purpose of your team and how you plan to serve them.
- *External teams* – Your team may need to coordinate work with teams outside your organization; the mission communicates the nature of your team's business and how you'll serve your external customers.

Your team may identify other people or groups who need to know about your mission. Make certain you communicate it to them clearly and thoroughly.

Conducting Ongoing Evaluation

You'll complete an evaluation of mission strengths and weaknesses — something that should be done at least annually and even more frequently for teams working on projects that change frequently. Your ratings help you identify strengths and weaknesses. This helps the team continuously enhance the quality of and commitment to the mission.

Evaluate your mission using the Team Mission Checklist. Then identify strengths and areas for improvement.

TEAM MISSION CHECKLIST

Circle the response to the questions to assess the effectiveness of your mission.

Our Team Mission is:	Responses		
1. Supported by all team members	No	?	Yes
2. A source of pride to the team	No	?	Yes
3. Easily understandable to outsiders	No	?	Yes
4. Specific and differentiating	No	?	Yes
5. Upbeat and motivational	No	?	Yes
6. Realistic and attainable	No	?	Yes
7. A basis for decision making	No	?	Yes
8. A springboard for team goals/plans	No	?	Yes
9. Supportive of a higher-level mission	No	?	Yes
10. A clear description of the team's purpose	No	?	Yes
11. A clear description of the team's customers	No	?	Yes
12. A clear description of team values about quality, service, and teamwork	No	?	Yes

Questionable or "No" responses indicate areas on which to focus for improvement.

Based on your scores and diagnosis, provide the information requested below.

Strengths	Improvement Areas

Now assign a task group to rework the mission so it retains strengths and the improvement areas are addressed. They'll revise the mission and present it back to the team for approval. This will help ensure that mission quality and clarity along with the commitment of the team remains high.

Endnotes

1. P. Pascarella. Is Your Mission Clear? *Industry Week,* November 14, 1983, 75-77.

2. W. Bennis & B. Nanus. *Leaders: The Strategies for Taking Charge.* New York: Harper & Row, 1985.

3. T. Peters. *Thriving on Chaos: Handbook for a Management Revolution.* New York: Alfred A Knopf, 1987.

4. D. Bradford & A. Cohen. *Managing for Excellence.* New York: John Wiley & Sons, 1984.

5. H. Mintzberg. The Manager's Job: Folklore and Fact. *Harvard Business Review,* July-August, 1975.

Chapter

6 SIX

Setting Sound Goals

> "Management by objectives works if you know the
> objectives. Ninety percent of the time you don't."
> > —Peter Drucker
> > Business Author

> "If you do not know where you are going,
> every road will get you nowhere."
> > —Henry Kissinger
> > former Secretary of State

The service team waited anxiously for the monthly customer satisfaction scores. It was Friday, five minutes past five, but no one would leave until accounting sent down the numbers. McKelvy was in the middle of an animated story of the credit department's latest blunder when the door swung open. Beth's face showed her exuberance. "Our goal this month was a two percent increase to 87. We increased five points to 90!"

The cheers and clapping were deafening and Beth had to shout, "That's a tremendous job. But let me say . . ." Beth waited until the noise level dropped to a few whispers. "I have to confess that I made a wager on this team with the branch manager. I bet we would exceed our goal. So we're on for pizza — Monday at lunch." The cheers reverberated in the small conference room. The level of energy and enthusiasm in the room made Beth's adrenaline soar.

A goal is a specified level of performance — the object of action. Quotas, performance standards, objectives, deadlines, budgets, and "to do" lists all are examples of work goals. The general term goal is used in this chapter and in most organizations to mean the same as any of the above terms.

It's a fact — people with goals perform at higher levels than people without goals.[1] But to be effective, goals have to have certain attributes. The acronym SMART is easily remembered and reminds us that goals must be Specific, Measurable, Attainable, Relevant, and Time bound. We'll discuss these attributes more specifically later in this chapter.

We'll also discuss how to set sound goals in ways that get commitment — you'll learn a proven format for setting sound goals and a process that involves the team members.

Finally, we'll discuss action planning with individual accountabilities. Action planning translates goals into the day-to-day actions which, if achieved, lead to goal attainment.

You'll recall the definition of a team from the first chapter — or any definition of a team for that matter. What's similar in all definitions is the phrase "common goal."

Common goals:
- Provide purpose, focus, and direction for teamwork.
- Motivate team members because they see themselves as contributing to a worthwhile team endeavor.

Without common goals:
- Team members flounder and the team is aimless.
- There is poor coordination of efforts and inefficient use of resources.
- There is no basis for follow-up and reward.
- The team has less-than-optimum team productivity.

Road Map

Behavior Model of Team Goal-Setting Patterns

The model of team goal-setting patterns consists of two factors: (1) goal clarity and relevance, and (2) commitment. A study of 75 teams shows that the most important ingredient of high-performance teams is that they have both a clear understanding of their goal and a belief that it embodies a worthwhile result.[2]

Goal Clarity and Relevance

Effective team goals are clear — specific, measurable, and time bound. They are also relevant — tied to important business results the team can reasonably attain.

Involvement and Commitment

Effective team goals are established in a way that involves all team members. When everyone on a team contributes to the goals, team members clearly understand what's expected and develop a commitment to working together in pursuit of the goals.

The Model of Team Goal-Setting Patterns in Exhibit 6-1 shows how team goals must have both clarity and relevance and the involvement and commitment of team members who must achieve them.

Below are descriptions of the four patterns:
- *Forming*: We have no goals or they are so vague they provide little direction and motivation for the team.
- *Storming*: We have clear goals but team members do not buy into them. Since they were developed top-down and handed to us, there's some resentment among team members.
- *Norming*: Our goals are not really clear and demanding — we are more concerned about developing strong teamwork relationships than developing and achieving challenging business goals.
- *Performing*: We work together to set "stretch" goals that challenge the team and motivate the team members. Our goals provide clear direction and strong commitment to working together as a team.

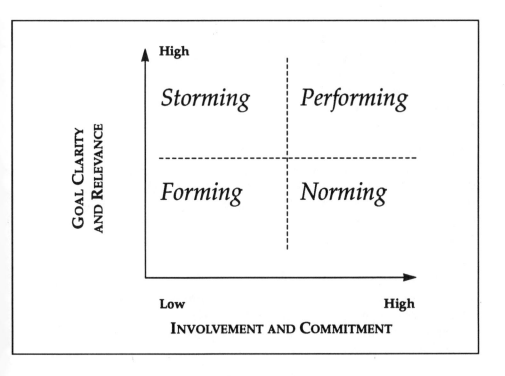

Exhibit 6-1: Model of Team Goal-Setting Patterns

Criteria for Effective Goals

Effective goals must be SMART.[3] That means they are:

1. Specific
The goals must be easily understood, concise, and unambiguous. They specifically tell what's to be accomplished by the team.
- *Specific* — produce 100 units with zero defects on the day shift
- *Not Specific* — produce 100 units

2. Measurable
The goals must be measurable so there is no question whether the team attained or fell short of the goal. Generally, measurement methods for goals include quality, cost, quantity, and time.
- *Measurable*   — reduce turnover by 20% in the next 12 months
- *Unmeasurable* — improve morale

3. Attainable

The goals must be attainable — neither too difficult nor too easy. Easy goals don't challenge and motivate the team. Overly difficult goals frustrate the team.
- *Unattainable* — reduce rejects by 95%
- *Attainable* — reduce rejects by 35%
- *Easily attained* — reduce rejects by 3%

4. Relevant

Goals must be in tune with the rest of the organization or work unit. For example, the team goals must be consistent with and supportive of long-term goals, department goals, team missions, plant objectives, expected business results, and the like.
- *Relevant* — increase production by 10% with no overtime
- *Irrelevant* — attend college class for credit

5. Time bound

The goals must be time bound. There must be time limits or parameters — specific deadlines for completion.
- *Time bound* — increase sales by 20% by December 31
- *Untimed* — increase sales by 20%

Zest Goals

Robert Schaffer, writing in the *Breakthrough Strategy*, argues that goals must have "Zest" which stimulates radically higher performance.[4] Pick one of your team's goals and give it the Zest Test on the following page.

Low Zest				High Zest
1	2	3	4	5
The goal is important but there's no real urgency.				There's a real sense of urgency. The goal must be achieved.
1	2	3	4	5
We don't feel challenged.				We feel a great sense of challenge.
1	2	3	4	5
It's just business as usual with no clear "win" point.				Success is clear and measurable.
1	2	3	4	5
We're just working in the same old way.				We're really working together to achieve results.
1	2	3	4	5
It won't significantly affect us whether we succeed or not.				The stakes are big. We'll be up if we win and down if we don't.
1	2	3	4	5
Nobody is willing to stick his/her neck out.				We're not afraid of mistakes; we'll try anything that might work.

Think of the last major crisis you experienced. The project was due in two hours and everyone pitched in to get it done. Everyone knew what was expected and did not let things like rank, position, politics, and working relationships get in the way of achieving the goal. This is an example of a Zest Goal.

Most people rate their most important goals 1 to 3. The exception are those goals that cause the team to "catch fire" — where ratings vault to the 4 to 5 range. These are Zest Goals. Zest Goals and *success* go hand in hand. The challenge is to develop goals that have Zest.

Guidelines for Selecting Zest Goals

Schaffer lists five guidelines for selecting Zest Goals — goals that are loaded for success:

1. Begin with an urgent and compelling goal — something which, if achieved, will make everyone stand and take notice.
2. Pick short-term goals or sub-goals — people should set their sights on a success within weeks or a few months.
3. The goals should be focused on specific, measurable, bottom-line results.
4. To ensure and engage everyone's commitment, the goal should exploit what people are *ready*, *willing*, and *able* to do — don't select goals on the hope of convincing people of what they should do after the fact.
5. The goal should be attainable with the available resources and authority.

Goal Timing

Team goals generally are short-term (spanning days or weeks). It's a good practice to develop short-term goals — especially with a new team start-up effort. Nothing is better for morale and enthusiasm than a few small successes early on.

If it is difficult to develop a short-term goal, establish a long-term one, then work backward. Ask, "What interim targets do we need to achieve in the next 4 to 6 weeks that will find us well on our way toward long-term success?"

Goals can and should be adjusted as the situation warrants — especially when things change, making the odds of success very low or very high. [5]

Periodically, at least monthly for most teams, goals should be examined to see if they are attainable and have Zest.

Elements of Sound Goals

Goals are the objects of action. So goal statements should focus on both — the action and object. Then the measurement methods must be addressed. Here are the three parts of effective goals:

Action (What's to be done)

+ Object (To what)

+ Measurement Method (How we'll measure the results — usually quantity, quality, cost, and/or time lines)

Action	Object	Measurement Method (Quantity, Quality, Cost, Time Lines)
Increase	Productivity	• by 15% • within quality standards • with no overtime • by year end
Cut	Costs	• by 15% • without lowering service • by September 30
Develop	New Crane Products	• two new cranes • according to specifications • within budget • by December 15
Solve	Quality Problems	• on lines A and B • lowering defects to 1:1000 • cutting costs by 12% • by November 18

Developing Goal Levels

Sometimes it is helpful to establish different goal levels such as "required-level" and "stretch-level." Doing so communicates to the team what's required for successful performance and also establishes a higher level target to aspire to. This "stretch" target provides additional motivation to achieve.

To establish different goal levels, first decide on the measurement methods — Quantity, Quality, Cost, Time Lines — that are required to meet the basic business needs. Then raise the bar a few notches to define the "stretch" level.

Measurement Method	Business Requirement	"Stretch" Level
• Quantity	• 200 units	• 275 units
• Quality	• 3% defects	• 2% defects
• Cost	• within budget	• 10% below
• Time Lines	• by March 15	• by March 1

Goal levels are perhaps most useful for experienced teams where their skill and effort can be applied to make a real impact on business results. The intention is to communicate to these teams what is "meets requirements" and what is "exceeds requirements." Simply the challenge of achieving the "stretch" performance level is enough to compel most teams to optimal effort. Ideally, rewards of increasing value are tied to attainment of each level.

Make sure the goal levels make good business sense. If the product is needed by the customer on June 15, it would not make sense to place a premium on getting the product out by April 1. There is nothing value-added for the customer, company, or the team with this "stretch" goal level.

Getting Involvement and Commitment

Here are 5 steps to get involvement and commitment in preparing goals:
1. Review the criteria for effective goals and the Zest Factors.
2. Discuss and agree on the Action and Object in a team meeting.
3. Ask team members to individually write what they think should be the measurement methods.

4. List the headings *Quantity, Quality, Cost,* and *Time Lines* on a flip chart and post the team members' measurement methods for Quantity under the heading. Reach agreement on the measurement method, then repeat this step for Quality, Cost, and Time Lines.

5. Compose the final goal and give a copy to all team members and others as appropriate.

Defining Goals from Actions

An alternative procedure for constructing short-term Zest Goals — goals that keep people focused and motivated — is to begin with action planning. Generally, people can quickly come up with actions the team should implement within a time frame like 30 or 45 days. Then, you can work with the team to develop the goal(s) that can be achieved if the actions are effectively implemented.

Here are the steps:

1. Select a time frame — for example, in the next 30 days.

2. Brainstorm actions — In a round-robin fashion, each team member presents an important action that the team should take during the time frame. A recorder lists the actions on a flip chart.

3. Discussion and consensus on actions — After all the actions are generated the team should try to sort them into like categories or combine them into groups. Then review each action to see if it is realistic for the time frame and is high priority in relation to the other actions. Reach team consensus on the priority actions and groupings.

4. Translate actions to goals — The team should review each grouping and ask, "Why are we implementing these actions?" The answer suggests the goal, end-result, or purpose that is to be achieved.

5. Refine goals and action steps — Refine the goals by ensuring they specify the action, object, and measurement method. Then finalize the action plan by adding other action steps as needed to achieve the goal.

6. Develop action plans — Define roles, accountabilities, and time lines for each action. Agree on who will be accountable (only one person per action) and the time line — when will it be completed?

Follow these steps and you will quickly develop clear direction, goals, and roles for the team.

Then, at the end of the time frame, review how you did and start the process again.

Endnotes

1. H. P. Sims, Jr. & P. Lorenzi. *The New Leadership Paradigm: Social Learning and Cognition in Organizations.* Newbury Park: Sage Publications, Inc., 1992.

2. C. E. Larson & F. M. LaFasto. *Teamwork: What Must Go Right/What Can Go Wrong.* Newbury Park: Sage Publications, Inc., 1989.

3. D. P. Slevin. *Executive Survival Manual: A Program for Managerial Effectiveness.* Pittsburg: Innodyne, Inc., 1985.

4. R. H. Schaffer. *The Breakthrough Strategy: Using Short-term Successes to Build High Performance Organizations.* Ballinger Publishing Company, 1988.

5. G. H. Varney. *Building Productive Teams: An Action Guide and Resource Book.* San Francisco: Jossey-Bass, 1991.

PART TWO

Synergy
in Action

Chapter

7EVEN

Managing Productive Meetings

"In meetings, when all is said and done,
more is said than done."
     —Source Unknown

C hris glanced at the clock. It was just now 2:00, the official starting time for the weekly team meeting. But their meetings never started on time, always ran late, and rarely accomplished anything important. Chris picked up the phone, hoping to reach at least two more prospects before heading out to the team meeting.

Chris and about a million other employees in corporations and organizations all across America share some pretty meager expectations of their workplace team meetings. Unfortunately, their expectations are usually reality-based, learned from experience. Precious few teams have mastered the skills necessary to make their meetings truly productive.

Do any of these descriptions apply to your team meetings?
* Too long and boring
* Controlled by the leader
* Dominated by a few influential or verbal people
* Poorly organized
* Diverted by people with hidden agendas
* Subverted by hostile and attention-seeking behavior
* Lacking focus on important issues
* Ending with no action

Are any of your team members guilty of any of these behaviors?
- Jockeying for position to push own views
- Droning on incessantly
- Sitting in silence, withholding critical information
- Dominating the discussion and railroading their ideas
- Backing down if their opinions are questioned
- Quickly agreeing with the majority position even without real conviction

If several of the descriptions are illustrative of meetings you've had, then this chapter is for you. So let's get started on making meetings productive.

Road Map

Behavioral Patterns of Team Meetings

The effectiveness of team meetings is directly related to how well the team *organizes* its meetings and gets *commitment* and *participation* during the meetings. These two dimensions and the four behavioral quadrants descriptive of the team's behavior in meetings are illustrated in Exhibit 7-1:

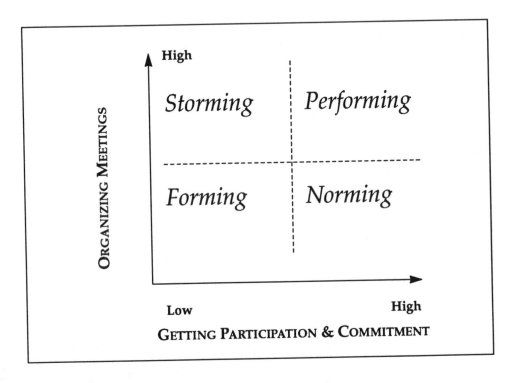

Exhibit 7-1: Team Meeting Patterns

Examine your allocation of points. If you see a lot of *Storming* behavior, your meetings may be organized but lack the participation and commitment needed for effective meetings. Or, if you see a lot of *Norming* behavior, you may get involvement and participation, but your meetings lack direction and organization. Exhibit 7-2 summarizes the characteristics of each pattern.

Pattern	Organization	Participation	Commitment
Forming	• Little or no planning • Unclear purpose • No structure	• Not encouraged or discouraged • Leader is passive	• Low • No action plans
Storming	• Clear, but imposed purpose/agenda • Dominated by leader	• Squelched and discouraged • Leader orders	• Low • Imposed action plans
Norming	• Little or no planning • Unclear or no purpose • Haphazard agenda	• Encouraged • Unfocusd, irrelevant • Rambling	• High, but uncertain • Action plans unclear
Performing	• Well planned • Clear purpose and agenda	• Encouraged • Full and balanced • Relevant	• High • Clear conclusions and action steps

Exhibit 7-2: Characteristics of Meeting Patterns

Establishing Meeting Working Agreements

Successful meetings are meaningful encounters in which people work hard, produce important results, and leave with a sense of accomplishment. Meeting working agreements, if established and agreed to by the team, can help ensure a successful meeting.

Here are some examples of basic working agreements all teams should adhere to.

Stress Attendance and Preparation

Place a high priority on attendance. You'll get it if your meetings are lively, involving, and productive. Also stress that everyone fully prepare for the meeting so time can be used efficiently during the meeting.

Be Prompt
Meetings should start and end on time. When meetings start late, the latecomers are rewarded, and the people who come on time are punished. When meetings run over, schedules are disrupted.

Follow the Agenda
Agree to follow the agenda. If other issues arise, list them for discussion at another time. It's the agenda that people prepared for and expect to cover.

Encourage Participation
Agree that everyone's viewpoint is important. Emphasize the need for active participation to share ideas, perspectives, and relevant information. Structure the discussion so that no one person dominates and to make sure that nobody is holding back.

Promote Constructive Disagreement
Let people know that constructive disagreement is not only acceptable, it's encouraged. This is because disagreement often produces creativity. When disagreeing, the individual must first fully understand the position being discussed. To test understanding, paraphrase to the satisfaction of the others, then explain why you disagree.

End with Action
Make sure all meetings (and all agenda items) end with a conclusion. The conclusion should include: (a) agreement on specific actions to take; (b) responsibility for completing the actions assigned to specific individual(s); and (c) deadlines for completion of the actions and follow-up methods for tracking the results.

Developing New Working Agreements
The list of working agreements is, at best, partial. Develop working agreements that fit your own team situation. Most important, when things go awry it means that you need to establish a new agreement to prevent it from happening again.

Don't dwell on what went wrong. Rather, acknowledge that something went awry. Then spend time discussing how to do things differently in the future and formulate a working agreement for governing upcoming meetings.

Working agreements are norms that the team establishes in a proactive fashion rather than allowing them to haphazardly form. If you let norms defining what's acceptable and what's not to *naturally* develop, rest assured that unproductive behaviors and practices will emerge.

lanning Meetings

An effective meeting plan establishes the purpose of the meeting, indicates what preparation is needed, and serves as a blueprint for conducting the meeting.

Responsibility for planning each team meeting should be assigned to only one person. However, that responsibility can be rotated so that all team members have an opportunity to plan meetings. Here are some planning elements to consider.

Defining the Meeting Purposes and Desired Results

In defining the purpose of the meeting, try to answer the question, "Why should we have this meeting?" For example:
* The purpose of this meeting is to finalize our team mission and determine how we'll communicate it to others.
* The purpose of our meeting is to decide how we can raise the quality of service we provide to our customers.
* In this meeting we'll provide information about the new profit-sharing plan.

Ideally, the purpose is motivating. If possible, weave in a benefit or two describing what's in it for the team members to attend (e.g., You'll understand how the new profit-sharing plan can be used to motivate teamwork and reward productivity).

To identify the desired results of the meeting, answer the question, "What should the meeting produce?"

The meeting purpose and desired results will overlap since the statement of desired results provides more detail about the meeting purpose. Here's an example:
* Purpose: Discuss team mission.
* Desired Results: A finalized mission and action plan for communicating it to the appropriate people.

Preparing an Agenda

Establishing and documenting a meeting agenda is critical to conducting an effective meeting. An agenda is a list of the topics and issues that will be presented or discussed during the meeting. Ideally, the agenda will also specify the action required (e.g., discussion only, decision required, information only) and show how much time will be allocated to each topic.

The task of developing an agenda naturally follows the tasks of defining the meeting purpose and identifying the desired meeting results. You would list the topics and issues required to accomplish the meeting purpose and desired results.

When preparing an agenda, check to see if you've considered the following:
- Purpose of the meeting. List the purpose (and benefits) of the meeting at the top of the agenda (e.g., presentation, discussion, problem solving, decision making). Knowing the meeting's purpose and benefits in advance will usually spark interest and increase attendance.
- Desired Results. Specify the desired overall outcome of the meeting.
- Set a definite meeting starting time and definite end time.
- List the agenda items with the type of action required for each (e.g., information only/presentation, discussion only, decision required).
- Determine the sequencing of agenda items. Most experts recommend placing the most important topics at the beginning of the agenda. That way, if the time allotted to each item runs out, only lower-priority items are left unaddressed.
- Set realistic time limits for each item on the agenda. As you address each agenda item, first establish a time limit. If time expires before the agenda item is completed, the team must decide whether to: (1) extend the time; (2) defer the item until later; or (3) assign the item to a task group for completion.

Specifying Attendance and Preparation

The entire team will attend some meetings. To other meetings, you'll invite only those who have some involvement with the subjects on the agenda — individuals who can contribute to the topics and people with a need to know about the subjects. Your selection of attendees for specific meetings should be based on the purpose and agenda for the particular meeting.

While listing the individuals who should attend, also list what they should bring to the meeting and/or how they should prepare for it. Then, when you announce the meeting, tell each person what he/she should bring and how he/she should prepare.

The meeting will be more productive if all attendees are prepared. Also, members won't be embarrassed because they can't participate fully. And the meeting won't be interrupted or stalled when people leave to get materials that they could have brought with them in the first place.

Establishing Meeting Roles

Team meeting roles should be defined and assigned for every team meeting. However, all roles may not be necessary for every meeting. Some meetings may need only two or three roles. The purpose of the meeting, desired results, and specific agenda items will help you decide which roles are needed for a particular meeting.

Ideally, roles are rotated among members so that every individual has an opportunity to perform all or most of the roles. However, roles should be assigned on the basis of the individual's ability to perform the role.

Several distinct roles are defined below. Your team may not require all of these roles. Or, you may need to define additional roles, depending on the nature of the tasks your team faces.

- *Discussion Leader.* This person guides group discussion. You can have the same discussion leader throughout the entire meeting or a different one for each topic on the agenda. The discussion leader may also record key comments or decisions on a flip chart for all members to see. Or this is done by the recorder.
- *Recorder.* Two definitions of this role exist: (1) take notes and record minutes of the meeting; and (2) record the team's ideas, decisions, questions, etc., on a flip chart during group discussion.
- *Participation/Candor Manager.* This individual monitors team member participation and intervenes to ensure that participation is balanced, with every member contributing and no one dominating the discussion.

This person also tries to make sure that everyone "levels" and contributes information that's complete, accurate, and constructive and not overly negative or positive. This role is particularly important when controversial subjects are being discussed and it's important that all members say what they really think and feel.

- *Time/Efficiency Manager.* This person's job is to keep track of time, periodically remind members of the time remaining, and ensure that the team uses its time productively.
- *Meeting Summarizer.* At the meeting's conclusion, this individual summarizes what was discussed, the actions that team members agreed to take, and team member assignments and deadlines.
- *Post-Meeting Coordinator.* This person copies and distributes meeting minutes and follows up on the actions the team agreed to take.

These are some of the roles team members can assume to help manage the meeting and keep things on track. Some of the roles may be combined and performed by one individual. Other roles may be defined as needed by the team in making meetings more efficient and productive.

Determining Meeting Logistics
Determining logistics involves decisions about:
- Meeting location, so you can reserve a meeting room
- Date, start time, and end time
- A list of needed supplies and equipment

Using a Meeting Planning Worksheet
On the following pages you'll find a Meeting Planning Worksheet with hypothetical team meeting information entered. It illustrates how you might use such a worksheet as a tool for planning meetings.

MEETING PLANNING WORKSHEET

Meeting Planner: *Sharon Johnson*

Date:

Time:

Meeting Purposes and Desired Results

Review progress: team project "X." We should all know where the team is in completing project "X" and the progress of each individual. Also, the Action Plan should be revised.

Agenda

Agenda Items	Action/ Outcome	Person Responsible
Introduce meeting and review agenda		SJ
Each team member makes progress report	I – Coordination	All
Report on copier machine decision	I – Features & Benefits	TH
Report on maintenance program	I – How it will impact you	BC
Assess overall progress against team goal	DO – Correction Actions	SJ
Revise action plan, based on above	DR – New Goals/Plans	SJ
Assign Tasks	DR – Accountability	SJ
Meeting Summary		SJ

I = Informational; D/S R = Decision/Solution Required; DO = Discussion Only

Attendance

Meeting Leader: *Sharon*

Invite	Ask to Bring/Prepare
Tom H.	*Material on Copier*
Bob C.	*Data on Maintenance Program*
Marie F.	*Progress Reports*
Susan D.	*Progress Reports*
John S.	*Progress Reports*
Bill R.	*Progress Reports*
Dan G.	*Progress Reports*

Special Roles

Roles to be Assigned	Assign to
Recorder	
Participation/Candor Manager	
Time/Efficiency Manager	
Meeting Summarizer	
Post-Meeting Coordinator	
Other:	

Logistics

Meeting Location: *O Bldg.. Conf. Room C*

Meeting Room scheduled and reserved? ✓ Yes   No

Date of meeting: *10/12/xx*

Start time: *8:30 a.m.*   **End time:**   *10:00 a.m.*

Supplies/equipment needed: *Flip chart. paper. and markers*

Meeting planning is complete when you've written and distributed a meeting agenda. Complete and timely agendas enable attendees to prepare, arrive promptly, and contribute to a productive team meeting.

onducting Meetings

If your meeting planning is complete, then you've laid the foundation for a productive team meeting. Now your challenge is conducting the meeting in a way that gets participation and involvement — efficiently and productively.

Participating Actively in Meetings

Team member participation tends to fall into one of four behavior patterns: *Forming, Storming, Norming,* and *Performing.*

Good participation is ensured by guarding against the *Storming, Forming,* and *Norming* patterns and using a *Performing Teamwork* pattern.

Participants displaying the *Storming* pattern can be expected to:
• Take over.
• Push their own ideas and put others' down.

Participants displaying the *Forming* pattern can be expected to:
• Withdraw or participate cautiously.
• Offer few ideas.

Participants using the *Norming* pattern can be expected to:
• Wander off on irrelevant issues.
• Offer irrelevant information.

Participants using the *Performing* pattern can be expected to:
• Participate evenly — provide his/her share to discussions without overcontrolling.
• Contribute relevant ideas — keep on track to achieve objectives.
• Offer new ideas — present creative concepts for consideration by the team.
• Encourage others to participate — present good questions and summaries; draw out quiet participants.
• Be open and candid — provide, analyze, and feed back constructive, complete information.
• Understand rather than argue — listen to the views of others and question.

- Clarify issues — reword and summarize issues to help the team understand.
- Resolve conflict — moderate disagreements so the team can get on with its business.
- Make the meeting effective and efficient — help the team achieve the meeting objective in the least time possible.

Assessing Meeting Participation

Using the following scale, evaluate your participation in a recent meeting by circling one number.

4 =	Strongly agree
3 =	Agree
2 =	Agree more than disagree
1 =	Disagree
0 =	Strongly disagree

Participation	Rating				
1. Participated fully in the discussion and made a real contribution.	0	1	2	3	4
2. Kept the discussion on track by presenting only information that was relevant — didn't ramble.	0	1	2	3	4
3. Interjected many new ideas and suggested actions.	0	1	2	3	4
4. Participated in a balanced manner, without dominating or withdrawing.	0	1	2	3	4
5. Encouraged others to participate by asking good questions and listening thoughtfully.	0	1	2	3	4
6. Was open and candid in presenting information.	0	1	2	3	4
7. Tried to understand others' ideas and opinions before arguing or stating his/her own.	0	1	2	3	4
8. Often clarified issues so everyone understood.	0	1	2	3	4
9. Helped resolve conflict and lessen tension when necessary.	0	1	2	3	4
10. Did everything possible to make this an efficient and effective meeting.	0	1	2	3	4

TOTAL: _____

Excellent = over 35   Very Good = 30 to 35   Needs Improvement = less than 30

Using a Post-Meeting Coordinator

The Post-Meeting Coordinator's role is critical to the follow-up success of a meeting. It's this person's job to follow through on assigned actions to ensure they're done — and done on time.

Another part of this job is also essential — copying and distributing the meeting's minutes. Every team member needs a copy of the minutes because they provide a tangible and permanent record of team activities.

Minutes should include written action plans which make implementation and further follow-up possible.

It's the Post-Meeting Coordinator's job to follow through on planned action to make sure that members complete their assigned tasks in a timely and quality fashion.

Conducting Ongoing Meeting Evaluation

To stay effective, your team should evaluate its meetings regularly. And if you feel the quality and output of your meetings are slipping, you should schedule an evaluation at the earliest opportunity.

The best way to conduct an evaluation is to ensure:
- Every team member provides input and improvement recommendations.
- The team discusses each team member's evaluation and reaches consensus on what opportunities for improvement exist.
- Action plans are made to keep future meetings effective and productive.

Have each member rate the meeting using the Meeting Evaluation located on the following pages. Tally the individual ratings to determine meeting strengths and weaknesses. On the basis of this information, determine what actions the team should take to improve meeting effectiveness.

Some teams keep a log of their ratings to track improvement over time. This reinforces the continuous process of evaluating and action planning for more effective meetings.

Meeting Evaluation

Using the following scale, evaluate each item by circling one number.

4	=	Strongly agree
3	=	Agree
2	=	Agree more than disagree
1	=	Disagree
0	=	Strongly disagree

Planning the Meeting — Rating

	Planning the Meeting	0	1	2	3	4
1.	There was good reason to meet, and the meeting objective/purpose was clearly communicated.	0	1	2	3	4
2.	The purpose, agenda, topics, and responsibilities were clearly spelled out prior to the meeting.	0	1	2	3	4
3.	The meeting was announced in a timely manner, and everyone was told what to bring or prepare.	0	1	2	3	4
4.	Given the purpose and agenda, everyone who should have been at the meeting was there.	0	1	2	3	4
5.	Everything needed for the meeting — information, supplies, equipment — was there and ready.	0	1	2	3	4
6.	Agenda items were organized with the most important topics at the beginning.	0	1	2	3	4

Planning the Meeting Subtotal (Perfect = 24)

Leading the Meeting	Rating				
7. The meeting leader ensured that the meeting started on time.	0	1	2	3	4
8. The leader reviewed the purpose and agenda at the beginning of the meeting.	0	1	2	3	4
9. The leader kept the meeting efficient and relevant.	0	1	2	3	4
10. The leader took steps to avoid any unreasonable interruptions or distractions.	0	1	2	3	4
11. The meeting leader kept the meeting on track and did not wander off of relevant topics.	0	1	2	3	4
12. The leader conducted the session so everyone had a chance to participate, and no one dominated the meeting.	0	1	2	3	4
Leading the Meeting Subtotal (Perfect = 24)					

Team Member Participation	Rating				
13. All team members arrived on time so the meeting could be started on time.	0	1	2	3	4
14. All team members focused on the tasks and issues without meandering, irrelevancies, and side conversations.	0	1	2	3	4
15. All team members cooperated to keep the meeting on track, use time efficiently, and record minutes.	0	1	2	3	4
16. All team members participated and contributed actively. No one person dominated, and no one held back.	0	1	2	3	4
17. All team members tried to encourage and support others to keep communications free and open.	0	1	2	3	4
18. All team members were very well prepared for the meeting.	0	1	2	3	4
Team Member Participation Subtotal (Perfect = 24)					

Meeting Conclusions/Follow-Up		Rating			
19. The meeting objective was achieved.	0	1	2	3	4
20. The meeting closed with a summary, specific conclusions and action plans.	0	1	2	3	4
21. Action plans and tasks were assigned — with deadlines; plans and tasks were recorded and distributed to all.	0	1	2	3	4
22. Someone was identified to prepare and distribute minutes.	0	1	2	3	4
23. The group paid attention to, evaluated, and improved team process — how team members worked together.	0	1	2	3	4
24. The meeting lasted the right length of time and ended on time.	0	1	2	3	4

Meeting Conclusions/Follow-Up Subtotal (Perfect = 24)

Improvement Actions

Transfer the subtotal for each factor into the column labeled "Points." Then determine your score: Excellent (E) = 21 to 24 points. Good (G) = 17 to 20 points. Needing Improvement (I) = below 17.

Factor	*Points*	*Score*
Planning the Meeting	_____	_____
Leading the Meeting	_____	_____
Team Member Participation	_____	_____
Meeting Conclusions/Follow-Up	_____	_____

Based on your scores and diagnosis, provide the information requested below.

What the team did well

_____

_____

_____

_____

_____

What the team could do better

_____

_____

_____

_____

Actions to continue

_____

_____

_____

_____

Actions to address

_____

_____

_____

_____

Chapter

8IGHT

Clarifying Roles and Responsibilities

*"Nothing is particularly hard if
you divide it into small jobs."*
        —Henry Ford

*"Everyone's responsibility is
no one's responsibility."*
        —Anonymous

Tom Wynne, Vice President of Engineering, met individually with the project engineers to explain their responsibilities.

For the next two weeks, two of the engineers, working tirelessly but in isolation, invested considerable time in the completion of their designs for the nuclear tube. Unwittingly, one engineer thought his task was to speed up fluids by X amount while the other understood her task was to slow down the fluids by X amount.

Wynne was flabbergasted when the two designs were brought together. "How is this possible — I gave each of you very clear instructions and you did totally contradictory work." Both engineers responded in unison, "I only did what you told me to do."

Role clarification entails establishing the responsibilities and roles of team members. Each team member must understand his or her responsibilities and coordination requirements — what he or she must do individually and with others if the team as a whole is to succeed. Each team member must understand the contribution and support provided by others as well.

Clarifying responsibilities and roles is one of the most challenging issues teams grapple with. This is because the source of most conflicts and performance problems can frequently be traced back to a lack of clearly defined roles.[1]

When roles and responsibilities are unclear, expect:
- Redundant and overlapping work on tasks.
- Backbiting and buck passing.
- Poor coordination and inadequate support.
- Lack of accountability.

This chapter addresses how to clarify roles, accountabilities, authorities, and coordination requirements. By clarifying roles, you'll avoid the situation presented in this amusing, but not totally unrealistic story:[2]

Once upon a time there was a work unit with four members named Everybody, Somebody, Nobody, and Anybody.

There was an important project to be done, and Everybody was sure that Somebody would do it. Anybody could have done it but Nobody did it. Somebody got angry about that because it was Everybody's job. Everybody thought Anybody could do it, but Nobody realized that Everybody wouldn't do it.

It ended up that Everybody blamed Somebody when Nobody did what Anybody could have done.

Road Map

Behavior Model of Role Clarification Patterns

The Model of Team Role Clarification Patterns consists of two factors — Role Clarity and Coordination, and Involvement and Commitment. The model in Exhibit 8-1 illustrates that team roles must be clear and coordinated and developed with the involvement of team members who must carry them out.

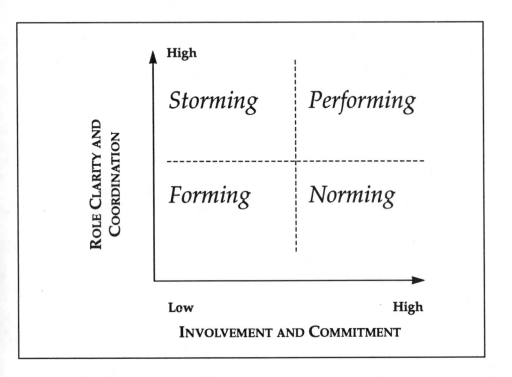

Exhibit 8-1: Model of Team Role Clarification Patterns

Team members displaying a lot of *Forming* behavior often lack clarity about why they and others are on the team and how they'll work together to achieve team objectives. As a result, there's a lot of cautious and guarded communication and testing of the waters.

Storming behavior is apparent when the team leader or a few dominant members attempt to clarify roles by dictating who'll do what, with whom, and when. As you might suspect, there's little commitment to adhering to roles that team members had little or no say in defining.

If you see a lot of *Norming* behavior, you generally have commitment to working together collaboratively, but little specificity in terms of role expectations, authorities, and coordination requirements.

A *Performing* team develops clear roles and responsibilities tied to specific team goals. The roles match each individual's interests and capabilities. As a result, the team is well organized, coordinated, and motivated to work together to achieve optimum performance.

Assigning Task Roles

Task roles are those things each team member must achieve if the team, as a whole, is to succeed. Each time a new goal is established or a new project assigned, the team should clarify task roles. They are easy to define but oftentimes neglected, as the tendency of many teams is to jump into a project with little or no planning.

To clarify task roles, begin with a team goal or project objective. Then pick a point in the near future — it may be one week, two weeks, or a month. Pose this question to the team, "Where do we need to be at that time, if we are to make necessary progress on our goal?" Answering this question defines an interim target for the team and the basis for working backward to define tasks for each team member. Then pose this question to each team member, "What do you need to do by when if the team is to achieve the interim target?" Once each team member has responded, the team should discuss the plan, make any changes or additions, and finalize it. A task goal description worksheet like the one on the following page is useful for defining the steps and tasks to be completed, by whom, and when.

Task Role Description Worksheet		
Interim Target (What's to be accomplished by when): **Follow-up date:**_____		
Task Description	**Person Accountable**	**Start & Completion Dates**

When to Clarify Roles and Responsibilities

Roles and responsibilities should be clarified when a new team is formed. Ideally, the right tasks are assigned to the right people — those with the skills and interests to carry out the tasks efficiently and competently.

Each time work on a new project or goal is initiated, role clarification should occur. Even experienced, highly developed teams should discuss roles whenever significant changes in circumstances warrant it.[3]

It's a good practice to allot time to plan task roles at least once a month or more often. This gives each team member a clear picture of what's expected. This also helps translate goals and objectives into more manageable tasks. As Henry Ford once said, "Nothing is particularly hard if you divide it into small jobs."

Once the task role description worksheet is completed, each person is given a copy. Now the big variable is, "*Will* each person uphold his or her agreements to the team?" You can help ensure that team members will follow through on obligations and agreements if you establish a follow-up date to review progress and completed assignments. Knowing that follow-up will occur is usually enough to spark team members to achieve their task assignments.

Clarifying Functional Roles

Functional roles help the team accomplish task objectives while continuously building strong working relationships. Functional roles were defined many decades ago, as early researchers clearly observed what team member behaviors help and hinder smooth and effective functioning of a team.[4]

There are two kinds of functional roles — those that help the team *get things done* (facilitate task accomplishment) and those that help *build relationships* (promote involvement, communication, and coordination). These roles may be assumed by individual team members or shared by different team members at different times. Both sets of roles are clearly visible on any high-performing team. Your challenge is to incorporate as many as possible into your own behavior in team activities.

Functional Roles for *Getting Things Done*
Roles for promoting direction, providing organization, and structuring team activities to accomplish tasks and goals include:
- *Initiator* — suggests or proposes new ideas or new ways of going about solving a problem or accomplishing a task. The initiator initiates procedures for the team — gets proposals on the table about how to do things more efficiently or effectively for the team to consider.
- *Information Seeker* — probes team members for clarification, supporting facts, and information related to the problem or issue being discussed. The information seeker strives to get all the relevant and factual information out in the open, where it can be used by the team.

- *Coordinator* — pulls together related ideas or clarifies relationships among various suggestions. The coordinator helps the team see common threads among ideas or how related problem solutions can be combined to form a potentially better alternative.
- *Summarizer* — restates suggestions or ideas offered by team members. The summarizer helps ensure that ideas, suggestions, and proposals presented earlier are given full consideration as the discussion progresses.
- *Recorder* — writes down or lists on a flip chart key points of the group discussion to ensure ideas don't get lost and to create a visual record of ideas. The recorder helps keep the group focused on the full range of important points of the discussion.
- *Critic* — evaluates the team decision or problem solution against a set of standards or criteria for "effective" decisions or problem solutions. Assesses the "rationality," "practicality," or "logic" of decisions, problem solutions, or actions.
- *Time Keeper* — sets time limits for various team activities and lets the team know how it is doing in terms of the time allotment. Helps the team determine whether to extend time lines or delay the activity.

Functional Roles for *Building Team Relationships*
Roles for promoting communications, involvement, and coordination include:
- *Encourager* — conveys understanding and acceptance of team members' points of views, ideas, and contributions. Helps promote active participation of otherwise passive and nonparticipating members by encouraging them to express an idea or point of view.
- *Harmonizer* — serves to mediate differences or reconcile disagreements among members. Reduces tension and conflict by getting people to openly discuss their differences, view things from other perspectives, and seek common ground.
- *Gatekeeper* (sometimes referred to as Participation Monitor) — keeps communications channels open and balanced by encouraging silent members and regulating dominant members. Allows everyone to get a say and participate actively in the discussion. For example, "We haven't heard from Pat, yet." Or, "How do you feel about limiting the length of our comments so everyone has a chance to contribute?"

- *Consensus Seeker* — sends up "trial balloons" to see if the team is ready to make a decision or able to choose from among a number of alternatives being discussed. For example, "We've discussed three alternatives for some time now. Are we ready to make a decision?"
- *Procedure Monitor* — proposes procedures that promote involvement, open communication, and active discussion. Intervenes when things get off track. The procedure monitor may intervene with a "process check" like, "We seem to be deadlocked — half the team is arguing for Option A while the other half is arguing for Option B. Can we take a time-out from our discussion and talk about how to resolve these differences?"
- *Candor Monitor* — monitors the openness of the group to assess whether people are saying what they really feel and think. Periodically may give positive and constructive feedback to the team or may intervene with a "process check" like, "Our discussion seems to be quite lifeless and guarded. How can we spin up candor and make people feel comfortable in openly sharing their views?"

These are just a few of the functional roles for facilitating group performance and promoting teamwork. There are many more complete sources offering thorough descriptions of functional roles.[5] Carrying out functional roles is often more difficult than it seems. Refer to the later chapters on Communication and Conflict Management for the specific tools and techniques for carrying out functional roles.

ysfunctional Roles of Team Members

Just as there are functional roles, there are also "individual" roles that are self-serving and detract from the overall effectiveness of teamwork. Self-serving roles that compete with teamwork include:

- *Aggressor* — displays aggressive behavior that puts people and their ideas down. May include joking, attacking the ideas or views of others, or degrading people.
- *Blocker* — is negative and stubbornly resistant to ideas. Resurfaces issues that the group has rejected. Disagrees or quickly opposes ideas without clear rationale.

- *Recognition Seeker* — attempts to call attention to himself or herself through boasting and continual reporting of personal achievements.
- *Playboy* — displays a lack of interest and involvement in the team activity by being cynical, nonchalant, horsing around, and the like.
- *Dominator* — asserts control by interrupting, forcing own views, giving directives, asserting a superior status, and so on.

These and other self-serving behaviors get in the way of or dilute the effectiveness of the team. They must be dealt with quickly and effectively or the team will squander precious time and produce disruptive conflict. We'll deal with disruptive, dysfunctional behavior in a later chapter. Here the intent is to help you recognize and avoid the behaviors that detract from teamwork.

Responsibility Charting

In work teams tasks are assigned, decisions are made, and team members execute the decisions and accomplish the tasks. On paper, it sounds easy. In reality, since there are multiple people involved, even the simplest task can become quite confusing and complex.

There is the person who does the work, one or several people who have authority to approve the work, and still others who are contributing to the work without having responsibility for it. Responsibility charting is typically used to improve coordination and address issues about *Who is to do what, with what level of authority, and what kind of involvement by others?*[6]

The first step involves constructing a grid; placing functions, activities, and decisions along the vertical column; and placing the names of team members along the top. The process is then one of coding each of the team members using one of five codes:

1. **R** *(Responsible and Accountable)* — the responsibility to initiate action, carry out a task or function, and recommend or implement a decision. This person does the work.
2. **A** *(Authority)* — the action, decisions, or function must be approved and the team member who is designated has the right to approve or veto.

3. **S** *(Support)* — providing logistical support and resources for the function or action. This person is not responsible **(R)** but must produce something that is used by the person responsible.
4. **I** *(Inform)* — this person must be informed about the plans, actions, and outcomes but cannot influence or exert authority over them in any way.
5. **X** *(Noninvolvement)* — this person is not involved in this function, decision, or action.

One way to display the responsibility chart is illustrated below:

Responsibility Chart				
R = Responsibility (initiates and is accountable) **A** = Authority (must approve or veto) **S** = Support (puts resources to work) **I** = Inform (to be informed) **X** = Noninvolvement				
Functions, Activities, Decisions	**Team Members**			

Responsibility charting is typically done with the entire team. Each team member completes a chart for his or her functions, decisions, and activities as part of a pre-work assignment. Then the team is assembled and discusses the key functions, activities, and decisions as well as how codes are assigned. For example, one person may report responsibility (**R**) for budgeting then code **A** under the department head's name showing the authority to approve. Another person may report responsibility -(**R**) for the marketing plan then code **A** indicating approval needed by the marketing manager and **S** indicating support required from advertising.

Here's how the responsibility charting meeting should proceed. Each team member reports on his or her pre-work assignment — the functions, activities, and decisions with accompanying codes. Next the team members ask questions for clarification — no value judgments at this point. A recorder captures all this on a flip chart matrix. After all the team members have reported and the team matrix is filled in, the team looks for gaps, inconsistencies, omissions, and the like and resolves them. The final product is clear responsibilities, authorities, coordination requirements, and informational needs.

Ground Rules for Responsibility Charting
There are several ground rules that must be adhered to if responsibility charting is to work. They are:
1. Assign **R** *(Responsibility)* to only one person. That person must initiate the action and is accountable for the outcome.
2. Be careful about having too many people with an **A** *(Authority)* function on an item. Too many people in charge will slow things down or cause deadlock as they try to agree on the item.
3. Look for one person with **A** *(Authority)* functions on several items. That person could cause bottlenecks to getting things done.
4. The **S** *(Support)* function is critical. A person with a support role has to share resources or produce something used by the person responsible. This support role must be clearly defined and the support person must commit to holding up his or her agreements.
5. Be patient — assignment of codes may be difficult. One person may want **A** *(Authority)* and not really need it. Someone may not want **S** *(Support)* responsibility but should have it. Finally, two or more people may want **R** *(Responsibility)* on a particular item but only one can have it.

Clarifying responsibility, authority, and coordination requirements can be tedious and trying but, once accomplished, team projects should proceed smoothly and the team should operate efficiently.

Endnotes

1. S. Buchholz & T. Roth. *Creating the High Performance Team.* New York: John Wiley, 1987.

2. S. Buchholz & T. Roth. *Creating the High Performance Team.* New York: John Wiley, 1987.

3. G. H. Varney. *Building Productive Teams: An Action Guide and Resource Book.* San Francisco: Jossey-Bass, 1991.

4. K. D. Benne & P. Sheats. Functional Roles of Group Members. *Journal of Social Issues,* 41-49, 1948.

5. E. H. Schein. *Process Consultation.* Reading, Mass.: Addison Wesley, 1969.

6. R. Beckhard & R. T. Harris. *Organization Transitions: Managing Complex Change.* Reading, Mass.: Addison Wesley, 1977.

Chapter

9INE

Making Rational Decisions

*"No good manager needs to be convinced that problem
analysis and decision making are the most important
things he does…His success virtually depends on
doing these things well."*
    —Charles Kepner
    —Benjamin Tregoe

*"Managers are regarded and evaluated
in terms of success in making decisions."*
    —David Miller
    —Martin Starr

Marion sat frustrated. For weeks, the team tossed around ideas about new product development with virtually no agreement among the team members. It's such a subjective thing, Marion thought. Everyone has a view and a pet product development idea. When we meet, people push their own ideas and criticize views of others. How do we decide about new product priorities?

If this predicament conjures up familiar memories of your own situation, you're not alone. Group decision making about the future is often subjective, speculative, and imprecise — and the process of muddling through the seemingly unlimited options can be quite frustrating.

Decision making and problem solving are among the most important applications of teamwork. Consider your own situation. How many of your team meetings are devoted to some form of problem solving or decision making? In this chapter we'll address a decision-making process that enables your team to make sound decisions efficiently.

We'll address two factors critical to good team decision making: structure and involvement. Both ingredients are needed to produce sound decisions that people understand and feel committed to.

Decisions reached by a structured process and with the involvement of team members yield:

- Better results — structure allows more information to be gathered, which makes for better decisions.
- Effective implementation — increased understanding means more effective implementation.
- Efficient use of team time — procedures and structure help the team focus discussion on relevant topics for the right amount of time.

Without structure, dominant team members tend to overcontrol and impose their ideas on the group. The team flounders and loses out on the thinking of the less vocal people. Without structure, decisions may not be processed in an organized manner; thus the quality diminishes.

When people aren't involved in the process, they often do not fully understand the decision; so commitment is low and implementation problems emerge.

So in this chapter we'll focus on how to make sound decisions — decisions that are high in quality and have the commitment by those that must implement them — and you'll learn how to have fun in the process.

oad Map

Model of Team Decision-Making Patterns

The Model of Team Decision-Making Patterns in Exhibit 9-1 shows how a team's decision making is related to how well it structures the process and gets team member involvement.

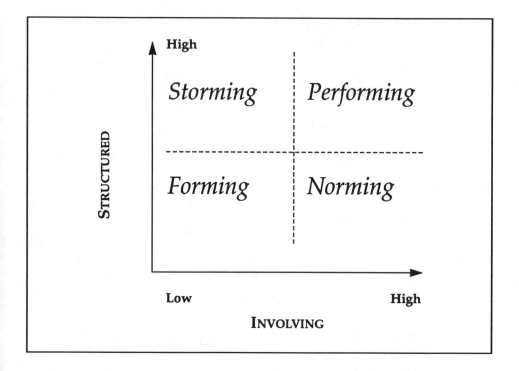

Exhibit 9-1: Decision-Making Patterns

Exhibit 9-2 is a summary of the four team decision-making patterns.

Individual versus Group Decision Making

A team generally offers more knowledge and information and broader perspectives than individuals making decisions alone — but not all decisions can or should be made by a team.

Forming	Storming	Norming	Performing
Structure Nonexistent Vague; unclear	**Structure** • Imposed • Decision may be predetermined	**Structure** • Loose; disorganized	**Structure** • High; good use of procedures by the team
Involvement Not encouraged or discouraged Unfocused, listless	**Involvement** • Overcontrolled • Focus on "who" is right, not "what" is right	**Involvement** • High; encouraged • Emphasis on "popular" decisions	**Involvement** • Full and balanced • Appropriate contributions by all
Commitment Low	**Commitment** • Low	**Commitment** • High commitment; unclear as to what	**Commitment** • High
Quality Low	**Quality** • Questionable	**Quality** • Questionable	**Quality** • High

Exhibit 9-2: Characteristics of Decision-Making Patterns

Here's a simple formula that will help you determine if the decision needs to be made alone or by a team:

$$ED = Q \times A$$

That is, Effective Decisions equal Quality times Acceptance.[1] Quality refers to the logic, rationality, and technical aspects of a decision. Acceptance refers to the buy-in and commitment on the part of those who have to implement it. Even a high-quality decision that has low acceptance is, by definition, not an effective decision.

Following this formula ask yourself, "Is there a quality component to the decision that will be enhanced if the team or a part of the team is involved, or compromised if the decision is made alone?" If the answer is yes, the team, or at least those with relevant information and important perspectives, must be involved. If the answer is no, then here's the second question, "Is there an acceptance component such that if the decision were made alone, those responsible for implementing may not be committed?" If the answer is yes, then team involvement is important.[2]

Determining if the Situation Requires Decision Making or Problem Solving

Before you start the process of making a decision, you have to make certain that the situation really calls for decision making — not problem solving. Decision making and problem solving are two very different processes and require very different procedures.[3]

The key factor in deciding whether you need to solve a problem or make a decision is time. The following illustration should help clarify the differences.

If your present situation requires you to look to the past for an answer, you should be problem solving. If your present situation requires you to look to the future for an answer, you should be decision making.

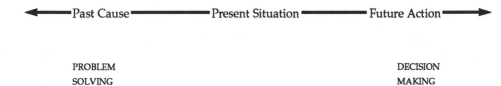

◄━━━Past Cause━━━━━━━Present Situation━━━━━━Future Action━━►

PROBLEM
SOLVING

DECISION
MAKING

Problem Solving

Problem solving always has its roots in the past. A problem is something gone awry where the cause can be traced to the past. Problem solving studies the past for the cause so that it can be corrected. By nature, it's more precise, analytical, and objective than decision making.

Precise
Problem solving is, or can be, a precise science because it seeks the one cause to a problem. It's tangible — it can be identified and found. There's little guesswork in problem solving.

Analytical
Problem solving involves investigating and analyzing facts — things that have occurred.

Objective
Problem solving is objective because it deals with facts. There's usually a definite cause of a problem; and if it can be identified, it can be solved.

ecision Making

Decision making looks ahead rather than behind. A decision is a commitment to a future course of action. Because decision making focuses on an uncertain future rather than a certain past, it's speculative, examining, and subjective.

Speculative
Decision making is speculative because it's an imprecise judgment call about which alternative is best. We're never sure we're right until the alternative is implemented. We make an educated guess, but it's still a guess — we're speculating.

Examining
The act of decision making involves an examination and study of information. We review the best available information to help make an educated guess.

Subjective
Decision making is subjective because it's based on judgment, debate, and future projections. It's not a precise science based on facts that can't be questioned.

ifferentiating Decision-Making
nd Problem-Solving Issues

Answers to two simple questions will help you determine whether to use decision making or problem solving:
1. Has something gone awry?
2. Do we know why something went wrong?

Has Something Gone Awry?

YES   –   Continue to second question

NO   –   Start decision making

If your answer to this question is *yes*, you have to ask the second question to determine if you should proceed with decision making or begin problem solving.

If your answer is *no*, you can start the decision-making process. Decisions are often necessary when nothing is wrong. For example, the quality of your products may be satisfactory; but you may want to make a commitment to superior quality. You need to find the best alternative to increase quality. You need to make a decision.

Do We Know Why Something Went Awry?

YES   –   Start decision making

NO   –   Conduct problem solving

If you can answer *yes*, you're ready for decision making. Once you know the cause of a problem, you're ready to determine the best future action to address the cause.

If your answer to this question is *no*, you need to find out why. Conduct problem solving before you start the process of decision making.

Review the following six issues and ask yourself the questions:

Has something gone awry?

> *YES* – *Continue to second question*
> *NO* – *Start decision making*

Do we know why something went awry?

> *YES* – *Start decision making*
> *NO* – *Conduct problem solving*

Then circle "Decision Making" or "Problem Solving" to indicate the appropriate process.

Turnover in the "X" group of employees has reached 15% each year, and something must be done about it.

DECISION MAKING   PROBLEM SOLVING

The copier we use isn't running and can't be repaired, and we need to make copies.

DECISION MAKING   PROBLEM SOLVING

Should we buy a new copier, a used copier, or use the one in "Y" department?

DECISION MAKING   PROBLEM SOLVING

Output on Line 1 has dropped by 10% in the past week, and we have to reverse that trend.

DECISION MAKING   PROBLEM SOLVING

Output on Line 2 has been consistent for six months, and we want to increase it by 10%.

DECISION MAKING   PROBLEM SOLVING

We need to develop a training program on the new computer program for the "Z" department.

DECISION MAKING   PROBLEM SOLVING

(Answer: Only items 1 and 4 are problems)

Four-Step Decision-Making Process

Procedures for making decisions consist of four steps:

1. *Defining the decision and setting objectives* — deciding the purpose of the decision and what a "good" decision should achieve.
2. *Generating alternatives* — identifying options that could meet the objectives.
3. *Evaluating, comparing, and selecting alternatives* — determining which alternative does the best job of meeting the objectives.
4. *Implementing the best alternative* — developing an action plan and assigning tasks for the team decision.

The following sections provide details on how to accomplish each step.

Defining the Decision

As defined earlier, a decision is a commitment to a future course of action selected from several viable alternatives.

The first step is to develop a short statement that defines the decision. The statement should answer the question: What are we trying to achieve?

The definition should be simple and straightforward. For example:

- *Buy a copier for the "Y" department*
- *Improve the quality of product "X"*
- *Increase output of Line 1*
- *Select new team member*

You can see that each example requires a selection from several alternatives. That's why the final course of action will be a decision. If there were only one available alternative, there would be no need to make a decision.

Setting Objectives

Setting objectives is the most important part of decision making. The statement, "If you don't know where you're going, any road will get you there," is absolutely true of decision making. If your team doesn't have a clear understanding of the objectives, you'll surely flounder or run into major conflicts in your attempts to make a decision.

Objectives provide the criteria of a good decision that help the team select the best alternative. Two types of objectives should be set:
- Mandatory objectives — objectives that an alternative must meet in order to be considered for selection.
- Desirable objectives — objectives that would be nice for an alternative to have — after it satisfies the mandatory objectives.

Mandatory Objectives
Mandatory objectives can also be called "must-have" objectives. No alternative is considered further if it doesn't satisfy all the conditions spelled out in must-have (mandatory) objectives.

Must-have objectives should have a limit — a quantifiable minimum or maximum. They're usually related to factors such as cost, size, number, and output — for example:
- *Should cost no more than...*
- *Should have a minimum output of ...*
- *Should be no larger than...*
- *Should operate on xxx volts...*
- *Should have at least three...*
- *Should arrive no later than...*

If an alternative fails to meet any must-have objective, it will be eliminated.

To reach consensus on must-have objectives, your team should answer these questions:
- What requirements must any decision alternative fulfill?
- What minimums and maximums will eliminate any alternative?

Desirable Objectives
Desirable objectives can also be called "nice-to-have" objectives. Nice-to-have objectives are things you would like to see in those alternatives that pass the test of must-have objectives. Nice-to-have objectives can even be extensions of must-have objectives — for example, the alternative can cost no more than "X," but it would be "nice" if it costs less than "X."

Desirable objectives don't always have numerical limits. Therefore, they are often more subjective than must-have objectives. For example:

- *Should be visually pleasing*
- *Should have an acceptable warranty*
- *Should require little service and maintenance*
- *Should be the easiest to operate*

Weighting Desirable Objectives

Once your team has set nice-to-have objectives, it should reach consensus on numerical "weights." This helps prioritize your "desirables" for later decision making.

Using the Decision-Making Worksheet

The Decision-Making Worksheet guides you through the process of making sound decisions. The sections of the worksheet are numbered, corresponding to the instructions below.

1. Mandatory Objectives

Write capabilities, specifications, or features each alternative must have in order to be considered for selection. Make certain each objective has specific limits.

1. Mandatory Objectives (MO) — List "must-have" features, functions, specifications. Set limits — maximums or minimums — for factors like cost, size, durability, time.
MO-1:
MO-2:
MO-3:
MO-4:

2. Desirable Objectives

List additional objectives an alternative ideally will satisfy, assuming it meets the must-have objectives.

3. Weight

Rate the importance of each *nice-to-have* objective on a scale of 1 to 5, with 5 being the most important. Objectives can be equally important and assigned the same number.

2.	Desirable Objectives (DO) — List "nice-to-have" features, and weight them from 1 to 5 where 5 is the most important.	3.	Weight (1 to 5)
DO-1:			
DO-2:			
DO-3:			
DO-4:			

4. Alternatives to Compare with Objectives
List each alternative in Section 4 shown on the following page. Write a brief description of the capabilities, specifications, or features of each alternative.

Compare with Mandatory Objectives
Compare each alternative with the must-have objectives and, in the shaded box, write:
- *Yes* if the alternative meets all objectives.
- *No* if the alternative doesn't meet all objectives.

Compare with Desired Objectives
Rate the degree to which each alternative meets each nice-to-have objective on a scale of 0 to 5, with 5 being the highest rating; then circle the rating for each alternative in the column labeled "Desirable Objective Rating."

Multiply the rating for each alternative by the weight assigned to the nice-to-have objective, and write the number in the area allocated for Score.

5. Total Score
Add the scores for each alternative. The highest score is the preferred decision alternative. This alternative satisfies the mandatory objectives and is the "best" relative to the desirable objectives.

4. Alternatives to Compare with Objectives — Describe alternatives and compare with mandatory and alternative objectives.	Mandatory Objectives? (Yes or No)	Desirable Objective Rating 0 = does not meet; 5 = meets totally Score = Rating x Weight
Alternative A Description:	If "no" eliminate	DO-1 Rating: 0 1 2 3 4 5 Score: _____ DO-1 Rating: 0 1 2 3 4 5 Score: _____ DO-1 Rating: 0 1 2 3 4 5 Score: _____ DO-1 Rating: 0 1 2 3 4 5 Score: _____ Total: _____
Alternative B Description:	If "no" eliminate	DO-1 Rating: 0 1 2 3 4 5 Score: _____ DO-1 Rating: 0 1 2 3 4 5 Score: _____ DO-1 Rating: 0 1 2 3 4 5 Score: _____ DO-1 Rating: 0 1 2 3 4 5 Score: _____ Total: _____
Alternative C Description:	If "no" eliminate	DO-1 Rating: 0 1 2 3 4 5 Score: _____ DO-1 Rating: 0 1 2 3 4 5 Score: _____ DO-1 Rating: 0 1 2 3 4 5 Score: _____ DO-1 Rating: 0 1 2 3 4 5 Score: _____ Total: _____

Example — Decision to Buy a House

On the next page is a completed worksheet showing how a decision is made to buy a house. This will help illustrate decision making.

As you can see, alternative A does not satisfy the mandatory objective for location and is eliminated from further consideration. Alternative C is attractive because it is new and has an allowance for landscaping and finishing the interior. But it is not convenient to schools and shopping. Alternative B has less than desirable wallpaper and window treatment but gets the nod because of more important features of location and convenience.

ecision-Making Worksheet

Decision to be made: Buy a house

Mandatory Objectives (MO) — List "must-have" features, functions, specifications.
- Set limits — maximums or minimums — for factors like cost, size, durability, time.

O-1: Cost less than $300,000

O-2: Located in Surbaban West area

O-3: At least 4 bedrooms and 2 full baths

O-4: Newer – not more than 10 years old

Desirable Objectives (DO) — List "nice-to-have" features, and weight them from 1 to 5 where 5 is the most important.	3. Weight (1 to 5)
O-1: Walking distance to grade school	4
O-2: Attractive wall covering and window treatment	3
O-3: Nice, well landscaped lot	3
O-4: Convenient to shopping	5

Alternatives to Compare with Objectives — Describe alternatives and compare with mandatory and alternative objectives.	Mandatory Objectives? (Yes or No)	Desirable Objective Rating 0 = does not meet; 5 = meets totally Score = Rating x Weight
Alternative A Description: olonial home on large lot near schools nd shopping mall. 4 Bdrm and 2 Bath. ocated on _East side_. Eight years old. ecently redecorated. Price: $275,000	**No** If "no" eliminate	DO-1 Rating: 0 1 2 3 4 5 Score: _____ DO-1 Rating: 0 1 2 3 4 5 Score: _____ DO-1 Rating: 0 1 2 3 4 5 Score: _____ DO-1 Rating: 0 1 2 3 4 5 Score: _____ Total: _____
Alternative B Description: rick ranch on 3/4 acre well landscaped nd convenient to schools and shopping. 0 years old with new screened in porch. 4 Bdrm nd 2 Bath. Located in West County. Price: $289,000	**Yes** If "no" eliminate	DO-1 Rating: 0 1 2 3 4 5 Score: 16 DO-1 Rating: 0 1 2 3 4 5 Score: 3 DO-1 Rating: 0 1 2 3 4 5 Score: 15 DO-1 Rating: 0 1 2 3 4 5 Score: 20 Score: 54
Alternative C Description: ew French Provincial on large lot with llowance for landscaping and finishing terior. West of city in new residential evelopment. 4 Bdrm and 2 Bath. Price: $277,000	**Yes** If "no" eliminate	DO-1 Rating: 0 1 2 3 4 5 Score: 4 DO-1 Rating: 0 1 2 3 4 5 Score: 15 DO-1 Rating: 0 1 2 3 4 5 Score: 15 DO-1 Rating: 0 1 2 3 4 5 Score: 10 Score: 44

Generating Alternatives

After your team has set its objectives, it will be ready to generate alternatives. Answers to three questions will provide most alternatives:

• What's available?
• What can be found?
• What can we design or develop?

What's available?

In many decision-making situations, the alternatives are already available and obvious. The alternatives may have been known before the objectives were set. For example, a team might know that there are only four manufacturers of the piece of equipment they're purchasing. Objectives are set to help the team select the best one.

What can be found?

Answers to this question are a result of the team having a fairly good idea of what it needs and knowing that many sources are available. Objectives are set, and the team is ready to start the search for the alternatives.

Assume a team is charged with the responsibility of purchasing a computer for its department. With the many different computers and types of computers available, the team should have an idea of what it's looking for before it starts to read the literature or visit computer stores. As more information is gathered, objectives may change.

What can we design or develop?

Some decision-making situations have no available alternatives at the time the objectives are set. So the alternative must be designed or developed to meet the objectives.

In this special case, the Decision-Making Worksheet is not used. Rather, the mandatory and desirable objectives are specified. Then, these specifications are used to design a program, product, or prototype.

Consider the example of a team developing a training program for the assemblers on Line 1. The team first sets objectives. Then, the training program is designed to meet the objectives.

Implementing the Best Alternative

Once the decision is made, the team must develop an implementation plan. This plan specifies to whom the decision is to be communicated and how it will be carried out. The previous chapter on role clarification provides useful tips on preparing implementation plans.

Team Facilitation

It's important that decision-making meetings be facilitated. Assign one person on the team to serve as the Team Facilitator who guides the process.

The ground rule for decision making is "objectives before alternatives." It's the facilitator's role to ensure that the team follows it. Most people would rather talk about alternatives than objectives. In fact, many people will have their "favorite" alternatives before any objectives are considered. The facilitator *must* guide the team to focus on objectives before discussing alternatives.

Doing Prework
Ideally, the team members are given the decision in advance and are asked to do three tasks as part of a prework assignment. First, identify mandatory objectives and be prepared to tell why they are important. Second, identify desirable objectives. Finally, develop descriptions of alternatives.

Setting Mandatory Objectives
During the decision-making session, focus on mandatory objectives first. Ask the team members to report their objectives and a recorder records them on a flip chart. After all the objectives are listed (with check marks for each team member with the same objective), the team should discuss them and reach consensus on the top four or five or so.

Setting Desirable Objectives
Repeat this process for desirable objectives, then discuss and reach consensus on weights. After the mandatory and desirable objectives are agreed to, the remaining steps of decision making are relatively easy. Most teams try to shortcut this phase and, as a result, get mired later on when trying to agree on alternatives.

Generating and Evaluating Alternatives

The next step is to generate alternatives and fully describe them. Then the team discusses whether each alternative satisfies a mandatory objective. Alternatives that satisfy all mandatory objectives are then rated against the desired objectives. The alternative with the highest weighted rating is selected.

Considering Decision Consequences

Especially on controversial decisions, it's important to involve people who will be affected — but it is impossible to involve everyone. A good practice is to examine the consequences and likely impact of the decision on employees, managers, other departments, people outside the organization, and so on.[4]

First determine who is likely to be affected by the decision and how they are likely to react — will they be supportive or resistant? Take this into consideration when making a decision, but do not choose a decision alternative simply because it will be popular or accepted.

Once you've made a decision and anticipated its impact on others, you can develop your strategy for "selling" it. You can sell your decision by describing the objectives it achieves and how it compares with other alternatives. Your worksheet is useful for this purpose. You also sell your decision by talking benefits — what's in it for the other person or department to buy into your decision; how will they be better off with this decision.

Decision-Making Worksheet

A copy of the Decision-Making Worksheet appears on the following page. Feel free to use it as presented or design your own worksheet to meet your unique needs. Using this or a similar worksheet helps the team structure the process and approach decision making in a systematic and logical fashion. Coupled with good facilitation skills and involvement techniques, you'll make higher-quality decisions that are fully accepted by those that must implement them.

Decision-Making Worksheet

Decision to be made:

Mandatory Objectives (MO) — List "must-have" features, functions, specifications.
- Set limits — maximums or minimums — for factors like cost, size, durability, time.

MO-1:

MO-2:

MO-3:

MO-4:

Desirable Objectives (DO) — List "nice-to-have" features, and weight them from 1 to 5 where 5 is the most important.	3. Weight (1 to 5)
DO-1:	
DO-2:	
DO-3:	
DO-4:	

Alternatives to Compare with Objectives — Describe alternatives and compare with mandatory and alternative objectives.	Mandatory Objectives? (Yes or No)	Desirable Objective Rating 0 = does not meet; 5 = meets totally Score = Rating x Weight
Alternative A Description:		DO-1 Rating: 0 1 2 3 4 5 Score: _____
	If "no" eliminate	DO-1 Rating: 0 1 2 3 4 5 Score: _____
		DO-1 Rating: 0 1 2 3 4 5 Score: _____
		DO-1 Rating: 0 1 2 3 4 5 Score: _____
		Total: _____
Alternative B Description:		DO-1 Rating: 0 1 2 3 4 5 Score: _____
	If "no" eliminate	DO-1 Rating: 0 1 2 3 4 5 Score: _____
		DO-1 Rating: 0 1 2 3 4 5 Score: _____
		DO-1 Rating: 0 1 2 3 4 5 Score: _____
		Total: _____
Alternative C Description:		DO-1 Rating: 0 1 2 3 4 5 Score: _____
	If "no" eliminate	DO-1 Rating: 0 1 2 3 4 5 Score: _____
		DO-1 Rating: 0 1 2 3 4 5 Score: _____
		DO-1 Rating: 0 1 2 3 4 5 Score: _____
		Total: _____

Endnotes

1. N. R. F. Maier. *Problem Solving Discussions and Conferences: Leadership Methods and Skills.* New York: John Wiley, 1963.

2. V. H. Vroom & P. W. Yetton. *Leadership and Decision-Making.* Pittsburgh: University of Pittsburgh Press, 1973.

3. C. H. Kepner & B. B. Tregoe. *The New Rational Manager.* Princeton: Princeton Research Press, 1981.

4. B. L. Davis, C. J. Skube, L. W. Hellervik, S. H. Gebelein, & J. L. Sheard. *Successful Manager's Handbook: Developmental Suggestions for Today's Managers.* Minneapolis: Personnel Decisions, Inc., 1992.

Chapter

10

Solving Tough Problems

"Problems are only opportunities in work clothes."
>—Henry J. Kaiser
>>American Industrialist

"A well-stated problem is half-solved."
>—Charles F. Kettering
>>American Inventor

Dana glanced at the wall clock and verified the time with the digital desk clock. In just 15 minutes the human resource problem-solving task group would assemble to address the turnover problem. The two hours allotted for the meeting would dart by.

The meetings were exciting and peaked the group's intellectual curiosity. Everyone seemed invigorated with the challenge of solving tough problems and felt a sense of gratification when top management accepted the solution and implementation plan which fully belonged to the team.

Dana grabbed the file folder and paced hurriedly toward the conference room. Unlike staff meetings, people were already eagerly gathering in anticipation of a lively and involving event.

Problem solving is at the very essence of a work team. Problem solving is where:
• Individuals working together bring different perspectives and information to bear on an issue that has wide-ranging ramifications.
• People pool their ideas and let their creative juices run rampant with more regard for quantity than the quality of possible solutions.

- Team members carefully weigh alternatives, looking for combinations and possibilities, and reach consensus on what they agree to be the most relevant, logical, and practical solution.

Unfortunately, it's not uncommon to find teams that:
- Get easily discouraged and lose interest because their attempts to solve an ill-defined problem are futile.
- Reject solution after solution until someone proposes one that, in relation to those quickly discarded, seems somewhat reasonable.
- Are dominated by a few boisterous individuals who forgot to leave their egos at the door.

In problem-solving meetings, teamwork is especially important. In this chapter, we'll look at practical tools and proven techniques that help teams brainstorm ideas, evaluate their merits, and reach consensus on problem solutions. In doing so, you'll have more productive and enjoyable problem-solving meetings.

Road Map

Model of Team Problem-Solving Patterns

The Model of Team Problem-Solving Patterns in Exhibit 10-1 is similar to the Decision-Making Model presented in Chapter 9. The model illustrates how a team's problem solving is related to how well it organizes and structures the process and gets team-member involvement.

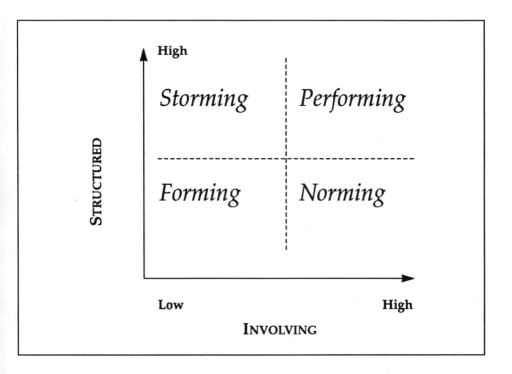

Exhibit 10-1: Team Problem-Solving Patterns

Forming behavior is evident by cautious, listless problem solving. *Storming* behavior is present when a few dominant members attempt to railroad their views. A team that's *Norming* is more concerned with the process than the problem. Finally, *Performing* behavior is evident when the team uses a structured process that fully involves the team members. Only the *Performing* team maximizes the quality of problem solutions and acceptance by those who must execute them.

Determining if It's a Decision or Problem

In the last chapter we cautioned that before embarking on decision making or problem solving, you have to make certain that the situation appropriately calls for decision making or problem solving. They are two very different processes and require very different procedures.[1]

The key factor in deciding whether you need to solve a problem or make a decision is time. The following illustration should help you distinguish the two processes.

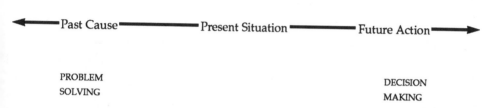

Problem solving always has its roots in the past. A problem is something gone awry where the cause can be traced to the past.

Problem solving studies the past for the cause so that it can be corrected. By nature, it's more precise, analytical, and objective than decision making.

Decision making looks ahead. A decision is a commitment to a future course of action selected from several optional alternatives. Because decision making focuses on an uncertain future rather than a certain past, it's speculative, examining, and subjective.

Answers to two simple questions will help you determine whether to start using the decision-making process or conduct problem solving:

1. Has something gone awry?
2. Do we know why something went wrong?

Has Something Gone Awry?

YES   –   Continue to second question
NO   –   Start decision making

If your answer to this question is *yes,* you have to ask the second question to determine if you should proceed with decision making or begin problem solving.

If your answer is *no,* you can start the decision-making process. Decisions are often necessary when nothing is wrong. For example, the quality of your products may be satisfactory; but you may want to make a commitment to superior quality. You need to find the best alternative to increase quality. You need to make a decision.

Do We Know Why Something Went Awry?
YES   –   Start decision making
NO   –   Conduct problem solving

If you can answer *yes,* you're ready for decision making. Once you know the cause of a problem, you're ready to determine the best future action to address the cause.

If your answer to this question is *no,* you need to find out why. Conduct problem solving before you start the process of decision making.

Who Should Be Involved in Problem Solving?

Generally a team offers more knowledge and information, creativity, and broader perspectives to tackle a problem than individuals working alone. But the question that inevitably arises is, "Who should be involved in problem solving?" The formula below will help you determine the answer to this question:

$$EPS = Q \times A$$

That is, Effective Problem Solutions equal Quality times Acceptance.[2] Quality is the logic, rationality, and technical aspects of a problem solution. Acceptance refers to the buy-in and commitment on the part of those who have to implement it. Even a high-quality decision which has low acceptance is, by definition, not an effective decision.

Ask yourself two questions:
1. Who has relevant knowledge, information, and perspectives that bear on the problem?

2. Who will be impacted by the problem solution and/or who will have to implement it?

Answers to these questions will suggest who should be involved. The final issue to consider is this: "How many people can we involve in the decisions to ensure high quality and acceptance and still have a manageable group?" More than 5 to 7 people will dramatically increase the time and logistical issues involved in group problem solving.

Six-Step Problem-Solving Process

Literally hundreds of problem-solving models have been designed for groups. Some are overly complex while others are too simplistic. The Six-Step Process adapted here is adequate to solve most problems.[3]

- *Step 1: Define the Problem* — Define the problem in a sentence or two.
- *Step 2: Brainstorm Possible Causes* — Brainstorm all possible causes and contributing factors to the problem.
- *Step 3: Collect and Analyze Data* — Gather additional data to verify problem causes and the impact on other people and work units.
- *Step 4: Brainstorm Possible Solutions* — Generate possible solutions with more regard for quantity than quality.
- *Step 5: Reach Consensus* — Use consensus techniques for reaching agreement on the solution.
- *Step 6: Develop an Action Plan* — Define the steps involved in implementing the solution along with time frames and accountabilities.

Defining the Problem

One of the best ways to define a problem is through Gap Analysis. Interestingly, this is a technique used by professional salespeople to help their customers see problems that the seller's products or services will solve.[4]

The most common conception of a Gap is shown in the following illustration, where there's a discrepancy between the current situation and the desired situation.

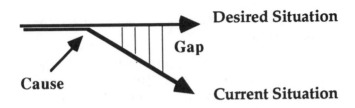

Thus, a problem definition consists of two elements. First, a description of the current situation or symptoms. Second, a description of the desired situation. The Gap will be obvious. Here's an example:

Half the shipments at the Biloxi Plant are leaving 7 to 10 days later than expected and customers are threatening to take their business elsewhere if the problem is not corrected *(current situation)*. We must eliminate customer complaints *(desired situation)*, or restore customer satisfaction through customer confidence that we can deliver on time.

Brainstorming

Before reaching consensus on problem causes or problem solutions, the team should have examined a range of alternatives. Brainstorming helps ensure that a range of alternatives is generated for consideration.

Brainstorming stimulates creativity. It induces involvement and generates excitement. Brainstorming sets the stage for high-quality, innovative solutions to problems.

The following procedures should be closely adhered to in the brainstorming process:
1. Set time limits for brainstorming.
2. Encourage freewheeling — go for quantity without concern for quality.
3. No discussion or criticism.
4. Encourage hitchhiking — building on the ideas of others.
5. Record all ideas on a flip chart.
6. Get input from all involved so everyone gets equal opportunity to contribute.
7. After the list is generated, look for ways of combining similar items.

Brainstorming Possible Causes

Here is the problem: *Over half of our shipments are late and customers are complaining.* Brainstorming identifies the following causes:
- The sales department is making unrealistic delivery promises.
- Orders are being processed too slowly.
- The plant is getting orders later than they should.
- The plant lacks sufficient personnel or equipment to handle the volume.
- Equipment breakdowns are delaying shipments.
- Snarls in the traffic department are causing backups on the docks.
- Line B is operating inefficiently.
- Production scheduling is off — some orders are early and others late.
- The Plant Manager at Biloxi is new and doesn't know the job.

These are but a few of the causes of the late shipments. Any one or a combination could be the real cause. If we do not do a good job of brainstorming a thorough list of possible causes, the real culprit may elude us.

Collecting and Analyzing Data

At this point your team may want to gather additional data on the problem and its causes. This may mean interviewing people, examining records, constructing Cause-and-Effect Diagrams, specifying Control Limits, and developing Pareto Charts. There are many good sources of information about analytical tools and techniques.[5]

Brainstorming Possible Solutions

Once the problem cause(s) are identified, the solution(s) may or may not be obvious. Brainstorming can help team members identify solutions that are not obvious. This technique can produce a broad range of creative and practical alternatives from which to select. It's important to follow the ground rules outlined earlier and keep the problem definition and causes uppermost in your mind when brainstorming.

Reaching Consensus

The objective of most teamwork activities is to reach consensus on decisions and problem solutions that reflect the "best" thinking of all involved. Sometimes the choice from among alternative solutions or decisions is clear-cut. Data may clearly show that one cause is the most plausible and the solution is obvious. Or, past experience may suggest that an alternative course of action will remedy the problem. More often, choosing among possible solutions is more subjective and requires a consensual approach.

Consensus may be a misunderstood term. It means finding a proposal that is acceptable enough that all members can fully support it and act on it in a unified way even though some individuals may have preferred a different solution.

Consensus is not:
• Unanimous vote.
• Majority vote.
• Everyone totally satisfied.

Consensus occurs when:
• Through brainstorming, a range of alternatives has been developed.
• The alternatives have been thoroughly discussed and evaluated.
• Through discussion and evaluation, everyone understands the rationale for the alternative — they may not be totally satisfied with it, but they are willing to live with it.

After all the alternatives are on the table, achieving consensus involves two steps:
1. Discussing the merits of the ideas, alternative choices, courses of action, — and then...
2. Reaching consensus through a process of narrowing down the alternatives, based upon their relative merits.

Discussing the Merits of Alternatives
After brainstorming, there will be a range of alternative problem solutions to consider. In this phase, those alternatives will be discussed and narrowed down. Use these procedures for your discussion:
1. Set time limits for discussion.
2. Allow each person to ask questions for clarification.

3. Look for opportunities to combine items.
4. Allow each person to voice his or her views on the pluses and minuses of each idea — those they endorse and why, and those they do not endorse and why.
5. Encourage differences of opinion.
6. Critique ideas, not individuals.

Reaching Consensus

After discussing the merits of the ideas, those involved should conduct a poll to select the most sound and important ideas. The following procedures are useful:
1. Combine alternatives if possible.
2. Individually, each person should select the top alternatives (e.g., top three) and report them to the group, along with the reasons for selection. Use a rating system where a "3" is assigned to the most preferred alternative, a "2" to the second most preferred alternative, and a "1" to the third most preferred alternative.
3. A recorder tallies the ratings. Then the team eliminates those alternatives with the lowest ratings and retains those with the highest ratings.
4. Discuss the merits of the remaining ideas and repeat steps 1, 2, and 3 above until a consensus has been reached.

Example

Here's an example where the group is using the procedure to choose from among ideas for improving customer service. The ideas were discussed and the group seems to be leaning toward Training for Service Personnel, Special Incentives, and use of Mystery Shoppers. The team needs no further discussion of Hiring Practices, Hiring More Personnel, and Follow-Up Activities with Customers.

Consensus Flip Chart

Ideas for Improving Customer Service	Bill	Karen	Tom	Denise	John	Total
Training Service Personnel	3	2	2			7
Special Incentives	1	1	3	2		7
Mystery Shoppers		3		3		6
Upgrading Hiring Practices					1	1
Examining Policies Customers Complain About	2				2	4
Hiring More Personnel						0
Identifying Follow-Up Activities (thank-you letters)				1		1
Developing a Customer Profile That Can Be Easily Accessed					3	3
Training Support Staff to be More Responsive to Service Personnel		1	1			2

Developing an Action Plan

Once the problem solution is identified, the final step is to develop an action plan for communicating and executing the solution. The earlier chapter on role clarification will help develop action steps, time lines, and accountabilities. The action plan should also delineate how the team will follow up on implemented actions to see if the desired impact is achieved.

Using a Problem-Solving Process

On the following pages is a Problem-Solving Worksheet. Using the worksheet will help the team develop quality solutions to problems that people feel committed to. Here's how you'll use it.

Instructions for Using Problem-Solving Worksheet

As you proceed through each of the six steps, you'll list *what* was accomplished and *how* the team went about the task. There is space to write *what* was accomplished — the problem definition, possible causes, data, and so on.

There are behavior descriptions for rating *how* the team proceeded through each phase. You'll rate behaviors that helped *Increase Quality* and behaviors that helped *Enhance Commitment*. Please rate each item, using the following scale:

SD — *Strongly Disagree*
 D — *Disagree*
 N — *Neither Agree nor Disagree*
 A — *Agree*
SA — *Strongly Agree*

After rating each step the team members should share their ratings and identify what was done well and what could be improved.

Using this worksheet as a guide, you'll help make problem-solving meetings more fun and productive.

STEP 1: Define the Problem

Increasing Quality

a. Everyone who might have relevant information is present.

SD	D	N	A	SA

b. A leader or facilitator outlined the procedures and ensured everyone understood them.

SD	D	N	A	SA

c. The Gap between the current and desired situation was thoroughly defined.

SD	D	N	A	SA

Enhancing Commitment

d. All members were encouraged to participate.

SD	D	N	A	SA

e. A climate was established so that all members felt comfortable in sharing their ideas and views.

SD	D	N	A	SA

f. All members were polled about their agreement with the problem definition and process for solving it.

SD	D	N	A	SA

We have defined the problem (Gap between current and desired situation) as follows:

Current Situation:

_____

Desired Situation:

_____

Gap:

_____

STEP 2: Brainstorm Possible Causes

Increasing Quality
a. The ground rules for brainstorming were reviewed.
SD　　　　　D　　　　　N　　　　　A　　　　　SA
b. All ideas about problem causes were posted — questions for clarification were asked with no value judgments.
SD　　　　　D　　　　　N　　　　　A　　　　　SA
c. The resources of the group were fully tapped to generate an exhaustive list of possible causes.
SD　　　　　D　　　　　N　　　　　A　　　　　SA
Enhancing Commitment
d. All members participated actively in the brainstorming process.
SD　　　　　D　　　　　N　　　　　A　　　　　SA
e. All ideas were recognized and welcomed — even those that initially sounded "foolish" and impractical.
SD　　　　　D　　　　　N　　　　　A　　　　　SA
f. Criticism and evaluative comments were discouraged.
SD　　　　　D　　　　　N　　　　　A　　　　　SA

We have identified the following causes of the problem:

_____

_____

_____

_____

_____

_____

STEP 3: Collect and Analyze Data

Increasing Quality
a. We identified sources of data that helped the team identify problem causes.
SD   D   N   A   SA
b. We developed action plans for gathering data that specifies who will do what and by when.
SD   D   N   A   SA
Enhancing Commitment
c. Most or all team members were assigned a role in data collection and analysis that fits their capabilities and interests.
SD   D   N   A   SA
d. Everyone felt part of the process and committed to helping the team solve the problem efficiently and effectively.
SD   SD   N   A   SA

We agreed to the following data collection and analysis tasks:

Data Collection and Analysis Tasks	By Whom	By When

STEP 4: Brainstorm Possible Solutions

Increasing Quality				
a. The ground rules for brainstorming were reviewed.				
SD	D	N	A	SA
b. All ideas about problem solutions were posted — questions for clarification were asked with no value judgments.				
SD	D	N	A	SA
c. The resources of the group were fully tapped to generate an exhaustive list of possible solutions.				
SD	D	N	A	SA
Enhancing Commitment				
d. All members participated actively in the brainstorming process.				
SD	D	N	A	SA
e. All ideas were recognized and welcomed — even those that initially sounded "foolish" and impractical.				
SD	D	N	A	SA
f. Criticism and evaluative comments were discouraged.				
SD	D	N	A	SA

We have brainstormed the following solutions:

_____

_____

_____

_____

_____

_____

STEP 5: Reach Consensus

Increasing Quality				
a. We thoroughly discussed alternatives, including the pluses and minuses of each.				
SD	D	N	A	SA
b. Questions of cost, short- and long-term impact, and other practical issues were fully considered.				
SD	D	N	A	SA
c. We focused on the alternatives — first discussing them, then narrowing them down, and finally reaching consensus.				
SD	D	N	A	SA
Enhancing Commitment				
d. All members participated actively and there was good pooling of ideas.				
SD	D	N	A	SA
e. We critically evaluated solutions without attacking the person and creating defensiveness.				
SD	D	N	A	SA
f. We constructively and effectively worked through differences of opinion.				
SD	D	N	A	SA

The following pluses and minuses were identified for each alternative:

Alternative 1: _____   Alternative 3: _____

Pluses: _____   Pluses: _____

Minuses: _____   Minuses: _____

Alternative 2: _____   Alternative 4: _____

Pluses: _____   Pluses: _____

Minuses: _____   Minuses: _____

STEP 6: Develop an Action Plan

Increasing Quality				
a. We identified action steps, time lines, and responsibilities for communicating and implementing the solution.				
SD	D	N	A	SA
b. The needed resources (human, fiscal, and material) were identified for executing the action plan.				
SD	D	N	A	SA
c. We established follow-up plans for reviewing the impact of implemented action.				
SD	D	N	A	SA
Enhancing Commitment				
d. All members were involved in defining the action steps and time lines.				
SD	D	N	A	SA
e. Everyone seemed pleased with the results of problem solving and excited about implementation.				
SD	D	N	A	SA
f. All members are committed to carrying out their roles and responsibilities.				
SD	D	N	A	SA

The team agreed to this action plan:

Project/Goal/Task_____ Page _____ of _____

✓ as Done	Action Steps	Person Accountable	Start Date	Finish Date

Endnotes

1. C. H. Kepner & B. B. Tregoe. *The New Rational Manager*. Princeton: Princeton Research Press, 1981.

2. N. R. F. Maier. *Problem Solving Discussions and Conferences: Leadership Methods and Skills*. New York: John Wiley, 1963.

3. L. M. Miller & J. Howard. *Managing Quality Through Teams: A Workbook for Team Leaders and Members*. Atlanta: The Miller Consulting Group, Inc., 1991.

4. R. B. Miller & S. E. Heiman. *Strategic Selling*. New York: Warner Books, 1985.

5. For more information about analytical tools and techniques see:

   R. Zemke & T. Kramlinger. *Figuring Things Out: A Trainer's Guide to Needs and Task Analysis*. Reading, Mass.: Addison Wesley, 1982.

   P. R. Scholtes. *The Team Handbook*. Madison: Joiner Associates, 1992.

Chapter

11

Promoting Open Communication

> "The number one managerial productivity problem
> in America is, quite simply, managers who are out
> of touch with their people and out of touch with
> their customers."
> —Tom Peters
> —Nancy Austin

> "I hadn't yet learned what I know now — that the
> ability to communicate is everything."
> —Lee Iacocca

Ralph's face flushed. "These people are all alike," he muttered to himself. "They are lazy, indecisive, and lack initiative. I don't like being dictatorial, but what can I do?" The team members remained silent — afraid to speak. Everyone could see Ralph's vice-like grip on the arm of the chair and his normally flesh-tone knuckles turning ghost white. The disgust and disapproval apparent on his face needed no verbal explanation. Each team member was thinking similarly — Ralph is so arrogant, belittling, control-oriented...and he doesn't listen. No wonder everyone is so cautious and guarded in their interactions with him.

What's going on here? Ralph, the team leader, blames his heavy-handedness on the team members and their unwillingness to take a stand. The team members see Ralph's caustic style as the problem. The real issue is a lack of good, open, constructive communication. Probably the most frequently occurring and difficult-to-manage barrier to effective teamwork is the breakdown of team communications.

Effective teams work through the breakdowns and develop open and constructive communications. Ineffective teams let communication problems produce undue stress and tension among team members which lowers productivity.

Communicating effectively means that communications are relevant and responsive.

Relevant communication is focused, concise, and task-oriented.

Responsive communicating involves a lot of give-and-take — there's a lot of probing, listening, and building upon the ideas and views of others.

Communications that are relevant and responsive result in:
- *Better teamwork relationships* — Team members develop satisfying and rewarding interpersonal relationships.
- *Greater productivity* — Teams get important information on the table, analyze and consider it, then use it to make decisions, solve problems, and get the job done.

Consider the individual who appears to have everything needed for success — intelligence, education, ambition, perseverance, initiative, analytical skills, and technical competency. Why does this person fail to perform to expectations? Certainly not because of an inability to handle the technical aspects of the job or a willingness to work long and hard. The problem is the ability to handle people — knowing how to listen, talk, write, present, and establish rapport. In a word — communicate.

This chapter focuses on the skills that will enable you to communicate more effectively. You'll improve your personal effectiveness and gain the respect of others with well-honed communication skills.

Road Map

Model of Team Communication Patterns

The Model of Team Communication Patterns in Exhibit 11-1 shows how a team's communications patterns are defined by relevance (focus, task orientation) and responsiveness (open, constructive).

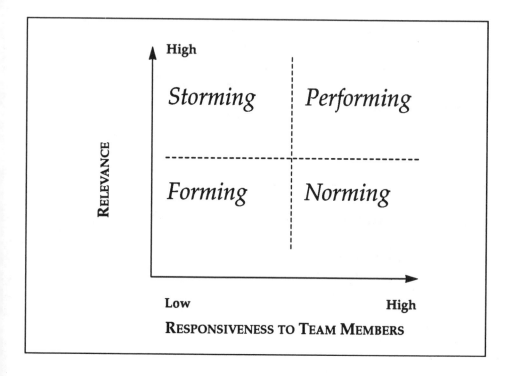

Exhibit 11-1: Team Communication Patterns

Exhibit 11-2 is a description of the four patterns and the results expected from each.

Making Assumptions versus Communicating

A good friend and skilled group-process consultant, John E. Jones, provided sage advice for communicating effectively in his paper: "A 'Vacuum Theory' of Assumptions."[1] This is how the theory goes...

Forming	Storming	Norming	Performing
Relevance	**Relevance**	**Relevance**	**Relevance**
• Cautious sharing of information	• Task-oriented • Focused	• Focus is more on team process than task	• Direct, businesslike • Task-oriented, focused
Responsiveness	**Responsiveness**	**Responsiveness**	**Responsiveness**
• Closed-minded, suspicious • Guarded, testing the waters	• Closed-minded • One-way, little probing and listening	• Highly responsive • Friendly, lots of talking and ensuring everyone gets a say	• A lot of participation • Two-way, open and candid, good probing and listening
Results	**Results**	**Results**	**Results**
• Little exchange of information	• Little pooling of information and ideas • Undue tension, stress, conflict	• Team development of relationships • Little emphasis on task issues	• Pooling of resources • Good confrontation and resolution of disagreements

Exhibit 11-2: Characteristics of Communication Patterns

When there is a void, a vacuum, a black hole — where there is missing information about a person or situation — we tend to manufacture information to fill in the blanks. Doing so helps us deal with confusion. After all, there's a natural human tendency to not be confused. We figure things out.

We figure things out about what others know, think, feel, and are up to. We make assumptions about how others will react, respond, and act. We manufacture explanations about why people did or didn't do something or behaved a certain way. In short, in situations where there is uncertainty — when there are information gaps — we make assumptions to fill them.

Think about your own situation. You have no doubt known others who have made assumptions about why Michael Jackson had plastic surgery, why Ross Perot dropped out of the presidential race, and how your boss would react if you proposed a drastic change to a workplace routine. In organizations where there's impending change like downsizing, rumors run rampant because, in the face of uncertainty, people manufacture information to fill the void.

Oftentimes we project ourselves into the situation, usually unconsciously, and read probable data, based on our experience. And assumptions that are unconscious are usually acted on as if they are true. There's a natural human tendency to see oneself as right. This is where the problem occurs; instead of testing assumptions, we act on them as if they are true. As a result, misunderstandings and communication breakdowns occur.

The probability of a communication breakdown increases with the number of assumptions left untested. In a team situation, the more people involved in communication, the more likely it is that numerous assumptions will not be verified. And the most threatening assumptions to the quality of teamwork are about others' motives — why the other person did or didn't do something.

The culprit in many situations where relationships have gone awry is a failure to communicate openly. Instead, we make assumptions and manufacture information and act on them as if they are true. Here are some tips for avoiding communication breakdowns and for continually improving relationships:

1. Admit your tendency to make assumptions and be aware when you do make them.
2. Test out your assumptions. Verify them with other people.
3. Clarify expectations of each member of the team and mutually agree on how you'll work together. Avoid the tendency to make assumptions and act on them as if they are valid.
4. When things get off track, renegotiate roles and expectations. Get expectations out on the table — agree on what you expect of the other and what he/she expects of you. In short, communicate.

5. Recognize that people are dynamic. People change, develop, acquire new skills, and establish new perspectives on things. Don't fall into the trap of thinking that the way things were last week is the way they are now and will be for the foreseeable future. Don't pigeonhole people by making assumptions.

This is not easy and requires effective communication skills.

Are You Communicating Effectively?

Did you say what I think you said, or did I think I heard what I thought you were going to say? The following illustration shows common communication breakdowns and misunderstandings.

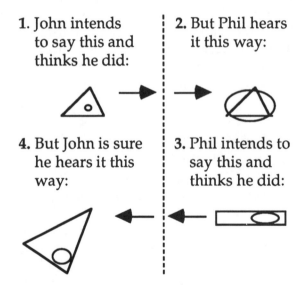

1. John intends to say this and thinks he did:

2. But Phil hears it this way:

4. But John is sure he hears it this way:

3. Phil intends to say this and thinks he did:

A single conversation is likely to end up with many different versions. One version is what you think you said and another version is what I believe I said. Both may vary from what we actually did say. Then a third version is what I hear and how I interpret the message to suit my needs. Finally, there's your version of what I said as heard and interpreted by you.

So when there are two people involved, the conversation quickly splits up into four versions. When there are three people, there can be nine different conversational patterns. When there are four people, it's possible to have 16 different versions of the conversation.

There are three factors that cause most of these misunderstandings.[2] They are:

- *Expectations.* People hear what they expect to hear or hope to hear. If there's a strong expectation for a certain message, then we bias our interpretation of the message in that direction.
- *Muddled Messages.* One person may have expressed a thought in vague and general terms, or even incorrectly. This invariably leads to muddled messages and misunderstandings.
- *Voids.* When we talk back and forth in rapid bursts of speech, we may leave out important parts of the message. Then, the other person must fill in the blanks — but they are filled in the way the receiver decides and not necessarily the way the sender had in mind.

The way to avoid misunderstanding is to establish effective, open, two-way communications. There are four elements of effective communication:

1. *Effectiveness in promoting candid communications* — the extent that people say what they really think and feel and encourage others to express thoughts and opinions openly.
2. *Quality of probing for information* — the degree that people probe for information and ideas that are relevant.
3. *Degree of listening for understanding* — not just hearing but fully understanding what others have to say.
4. *Clarity of presenting information and ideas* — the extent that people provide information and ideas in a way that others fully understand.

The following sections provide details on each aspect.

Promoting Candid Communications

Communicating candidly and honestly means telling others what you really think and feel — spelling out your views clearly, completely, and constructively. When you're honest and candid, you're telling the team, in effect, "This is what I actually think and feel on this topic."

Being candid isn't easy. We've all been conditioned to say something "nice" or what's "expected" instead of being candid. However, effective teamwork depends on the team being open — freely sharing information and viewpoints.

Guidelines for Candid Communications

There are four important guidelines for communicating more openly and candidly:

1. *Be willing to fully express your views* — Team members who are willing to fully disclose their views are more likely to be effective communicators and contribute to the team effort. Other members of the team want to know where you're coming from. Tell them. Make a conscious effort to communicate your true feelings and ideas about the topic.

   Go beyond simply exchanging information. Express your honest feelings about the topic under discussion. In doing so, you'll encourage others to be candid as well.

2. *Avoid becoming angry or annoyed when another person's views differ from yours* — You tell others a lot about yourself by the way you respond to opposing views. If you get angry or appear threatened every time an opposing view is offered, others will avoid disagreeing with you and may even be reluctant to work with you. As a result, communication is "no-way" — some potentially good ideas may never be considered.

   Try to understand the other person's views. Remember, perceptions are neither "right" nor "wrong." They simply exist and must be managed.

3. *Be willing to change your views as new information becomes available* — Too often, we believe we have a "lock" on the truth. Since our views are obviously correct, then any opposing views must be incorrect.

   One of the greatest challenges for team members is to keep an open mind. Hear others out and try to understand their views — especially when they differ from yours. You may gain some insight that will help you improve your effectiveness.

4. *Think win-win* — You may think only in terms of winning or losing when there are disagreements and opposing views. If you do, there will be a winner and a loser. Coming out on top may give your ego a boost in the short term, but the long-term result will be damaged relationships; and you're likely to lose the respect of the team members.

Don't get trapped in a win-lose mentality. Try to understand where other people are coming from, and help them understand where you're coming from. Focus on the objective, goal, or result you're mutually pursuing, not on winning or losing.

Follow these guidelines whenever you're communicating with team members. You'll find that as your candor increases, other team members become more candid as well. More candid communications result in more productive and enjoyable teamwork.

Take a Candor Check

It is helpful to periodically take a candor rating on your team. That way you can determine the current level of candor and take the required action to spin it up. Here are the steps:

1. Individually respond to the communication factors on the candor check-up appearing on the following page. Then take turns reporting your evaluations to the team.
2. A recorder should summarize the ratings on a flip chart like the one below:

Communication Factor	Individual Ratings	Average
• **My Candor**	4 4 5 3 3 4	3.83
• **Their Candor**	1 2 2 3 2 3	2.16
• **Quality of Probing**	2 3 2 3 4 1	2.50
• **Quality of Listening**	2 3 3 3 4 3	3.00
• **Pooling of Ideas**	3 2 2 3 2 2	2.33

3. As a team, review the candor ratings and diagnose what is going on. Determine what the team is doing that's effective and ineffective. Which areas are low and high? Is there a difference between "My Candor" and "Their Candor"?
4. Determine some immediate actions to improve candor and communications.

Candor Check-Up

Please rate the Communication Factors below using the following scale:

- 5 — To a very great extent; no improvement needed
- 4 — To a great extent; little improvement needed
- 3 — To some extent; some improvement needed
- 2 — To a little extent; significant improvement needed
- 1 — To a very little extent; substantial improvement needed

Communication Factors	My Rating *Circle one*	Team Ratings *Please list*
My Candor — the extent that I am saying what I really think and feel	1 2 3 4 5	
Their Candor— the extent that others are being candid	1 2 3 4 5	
Quality of Probing — the extent that the team members are probing one another's views and ideas	1 2 3 4 5	
Quality of Listening — the extent that the team members are listening to one another	1 2 3 4 5	
Pooling of Information — the extent that the team is building on the ideas and information of others	1 2 3 4 5	

Strengths to Maintain or Build Upon:

Suggestions for Improvement:

Probing for Information

Your role as a team member is to provide and draw out from others information that is critical to the subject being discussed. Most of us are more effective at presenting our own views than drawing out information from others.

A good name for the skill of gathering information from others is probing.[3] You use different probes in your daily communications without being aware of them.

When you probe, you:
- *Get others involved and participating* — Since probes are designed to produce a response, it's unlikely that the other person will remain passive.
- *Get important information on the table* — People may not volunteer information, or the ideas they present may not be clear. Your probes help people open up, present their information, or clarify their ideas.
- *Force yourself to listen* — Since probes are most effective in a sequence, you have to listen to a person's response.
- *Improve team relationships* — When you use probes effectively, you help improve communications among all team members; better communications mean better interpersonal relations.

Types of Probes

There are five probes that help you draw out information and ideas from team members: Open Probes; Pauses; Reflective Statements; Summary Probes; and Fact-Finding Questions.

Think of a funnel with the probes arranged from the lip to the spout, as in Exhibit 11-3. This gives you an idea of how probes work. The open probe allows the greatest amount of information to flow. It's the least restrictive.

The fact-finding probe is the most restrictive since it gathers simple responses like "yes" or "no" or some factual response. The others fall in between in terms of the amount of information they yield.

The probes are explained on the following pages.

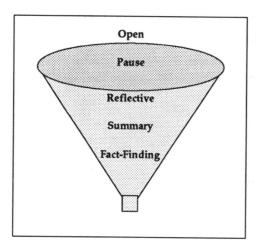

Exhibit 11-3: Probe Funnel

Probe Definitions

Open

Definition	Objectives	Characteristics	Examples
A question or statement that invites a wide-ranging response; often asks for ideas, opinions, or views	• Open up discussion • Invite broad-ranging responses • Give other freedom to say what's on his/her mind • Help get other involved	• Can't be answered "yes" or "no" • Often starts with "What," "Why," "Tell me," "How" • Gets at feelings, opinions, thoughts	• "What do you think about...?" • "How is it that...?" • "Tell me about..." • "Why do you think...?" • "What's your opinion on...?"

Pause

Definition	Objectives	Characteristics	Examples
An intentional, purposeful period of silence	• Give other a chance to think • Allow other time to respond • Slow down pace of a talk • Draw out other person's silence	• Usually follows questions • Deliberate *(Not a probe when you're at a loss for words)*	• _____ • "Why do you say that?_____"

Reflective

Definition	Objectives	Characteristics	Examples
A statement that describes and reflects a feeling or emotion (without implying agreement or disagreement)	• Identify feelings or emotions • Show you understand • Vent interfering emotions • Invite expressions of feeling and refocus thinking	• Names a feeling or emotion • Usually uses the word "you" or "you're"	• "You're pretty mad about it." • "You seem to be reluctant to talk about the problem." • "That sounds exciting!" • "I can tell it's getting to you."

Summary

Definition	Objectives	Characteristics	Examples
A brief restatement, in your own words, of the content of what was said	• Check your understanding • Prove you're listening • Give structure and direction to a talk • Help other clarify his/her own thinking • Invite other to comment or expand	• Summarizes a content, not feelings • Restates essential ideas • Uses other's own words • May start with introductory comment	• "So, you disagree about..." • "The way you see it is..." • "You prefer working overtime." • "Let me summarize my understanding..."

Fact-Finding

Definition	Objectives	Characteristics	Examples
A question that limits the answer by requesting specific facts or a "yes" or "no" answer	• Find out details, specifics • Check out understanding • Direct the discussion • Get other to take a stand	• Often starts with "Who," "Which," "When," "Where," "How many," etc. • Can sometimes be answered with a simple "yes" or "no"	• "Who is in charge of...?" • "Which work order...?" • "When will you be able...?" • "Can we talk about...?" • "Do you think...?"

Team members who are considered "effective" communicators use a variety of probes. They balance open probes with fact-finding probes. They pause to let others consider the questions, formulate a response, and then respond. They periodically summarize what was heard to check understanding.

"Effective" communicators also tailor their probes to the particular individual they are dealing with. For example, if you're working with a very reserved person, using a lot of open probes and pauses will help get them to open up. If you have a very talkative person, containing the discussion with more fact-finding questions is appropriate.

A Caution: Fact-Finding Probes that Become Leading Questions

Be careful in using fact-finding probes. You'll obviously need to use them when you want a factual or *yes* or *no* answer.

A problem with fact-finding probes is that they often turn into leading questions — probes that clearly telegraph the answer you want. The answer is built into or implied by the question, so leading questions actually lead or force the answer the questioner wants to hear. Examples of leading questions are:

- *"You don't want people to think you're stupid, do you?"*
- *"That's really a good idea, isn't it?"*
- *"You don't really think it will work, do you?"*

When you use leading questions properly, they can help you confirm understanding or get agreement. When you use them improperly, leading questions make others feel you're trying to force your views on them by putting words in their mouths.

Listening for Understanding

The ability to *really* listen is an important skill in any interaction with people. Listening allows you to understand where the other person is coming from and shows you're interested in what he or she has to say.

By listening to and understanding what the other person has to say, you're basically communicating: "You're important, and what you have to say is of value to me."

Common Listening Problems

Unfortunately, we all experience several common listening problems:

- *Letting attention wander* — Good listening requires more effort than most of us are willing to put forth.
- *Missing the real point* — Sometimes we listen carefully, concentrate on the facts, even write them down; yet we don't hear, or we misunderstand the real message.
- *Letting emotions interfere* — Emotions are barriers to listening. If we get angry or too enthusiastic, we can't fully comprehend what is being said.
- *"Stepping on" another person's statements* — We're sometimes so eager to get on with our own talking that we "step on" the other's statements. Rather than hearing the other person out, we're quick to set them right with our wisdom on the topic.
- *Thinking ahead* — We think much faster than we speak. If we speak 120 to 160 words a minute, we think four or five times that speed. By thinking ahead, we try to anticipate what the other person will say and cut him or her off prematurely.

To see if you have these and other listening problems, complete the Listening Skills Evaluation below. Circle your response for each item.

Do you frequently:

• Interrupt others?	**Yes**	**No**
• Show impatience as you wait for others to finish speaking?	**Yes**	**No**
• Spend more time talking than listening?	**Yes**	**No**
• Find that your mind wanders and makes you miss parts of what others are saying?	**Yes**	**No**
• Think about what you're going to say next instead of paying attention to what the other person is saying?	**Yes**	**No**
• Demonstrate nonverbally, through signals like poor eye contact and bored expressions, that you're not interested in what's being said?	**Yes**	**No**
• Find yourself finishing the sentences of other people?	**Yes**	**No**

Each *Yes* you circled indicates an area in which improvement may be useful. Study the following guidelines for improving your listening skills for helpful hints.

Guidelines for Improving Listening Skills

Follow the guidelines below to improve your listening skills and overcome listening problems:

- *Decide to listen* — Make a conscious effort to limit your talking to one minute or less; then ask a question of the other person. During a discussion, think about how well you're listening. After a discussion, evaluate how well you listened.
- *Give your undivided attention* — Discipline yourself to practice focusing full attention on what the other person is saying. Remember that people dislike being ignored.
- *Control your emotions* — Don't let your emotions close your mind. Anger, excitement, and anxiety all get in the way of good listening. Acknowledge your emotion; ask for a break and calm down.
- *Listen for meaning* — Listen beyond the facts for meaning. Ask yourself, "What is this person really trying to say?" Probe for clarification or to draw out the real message.
- *Feed back what you've heard* — Repeat what you've heard, and ask if your version is correct. This technique, called feedback, shows the other person that you're interested and prompts a correction if required. Feedback forces you to listen and ensures you've understood what the other person is saying.
- *Postpone evaluation* — Discipline yourself not to evaluate until you fully understand and have considered an idea's merits. When ideas are presented, many people are too quick to evaluate the idea. They judge it as either good or bad before they really understand the idea and carefully consider it; they stop listening to what the other person is saying.

esenting Information and Ideas

Another aspect of effective communications is presenting your own information and ideas. Your ability to present information to others is just as critical to the team's success as your ability to speak candidly, gather information from others, and listen.

Other team members depend on the information and ideas you can provide. When you don't present your ideas effectively, team members don't have the chance to give your ideas the consideration they deserve.

Methods for Improving Your Presentation Skills

The following methods will help improve your ability to present information and ideas:

- *Express your thoughts clearly and concisely* — Organize your thoughts. Think through what you plan to say before you say it. Think of the listener; choose words that make it easier for the listener to understand. Be thorough but concise.
- *Make one point at a time* — Ideas are easier to digest if you present one at a time. A barrage of ideas can be intimidating. After making your point, pause to let it sink in.
- *Check for understanding* — Don't assume that the other person understands what you said. Probe. Ask for a summary or reaction to make sure the listener heard what you said. For example, "Am I being clear?" or, "Do you understand?"
- *Clarify when necessary* — The person you're presenting to will tell you if this step is needed. The response you get when you check for understanding determines whether you need to clarify what you're saying. If you do need to clarify what you said, make sure you check for understanding again.
- *Get a reaction* — Once you know you've explained your idea fully, ask for the other person's reaction — for example, "How do you feel about what I've proposed?"
  Be prepared for an ambiguous answer like, "I'll have to think about it." Give the other person as much time as you think you would need to decide how you feel about an idea.
- *Balance presenting and listening* — Promote two-way communication by making a conscious effort to balance the time you spend talking and listening.

resenting with Impact

Any salesperson will tell you, "People don't buy things, they buy what the things will do for them."[4] They buy the "wiifm" — *what's in it for me.* So if the purpose of your communication is to persuade, influence, and get buy-in, you need to talk *wiifm* when you present information to others.

Wiifm spells out the benefits for the other person to go along with your proposal. Here's how to develop a *wiifm* statement:

State Need + Describe Feature + Describe Function + Show Benefit (wiifm) + Check for Acceptance

State Need:
"You said you wanted to reduce costs."

Describe Feature:
"An important feature of workflow analysis is Process Mapping."

Describe Function:
"Process Mapping charts the flow of work including major decisions, activities, delays, inspections, and transporting."

Show Benefit (wiifm):
"By using a process map, you'll identify duplications, non-value-added activities, and delays which, if dealt with properly, will produce substantial cost savings."

Check for Acceptance:
"How does that strike you?"

Wiifm statements are powerful. They help you tailor your presentation to meet the unique needs of others and show how they will be better off with what you propose. If you are giving a presentation where the goal is persuasion, make sure it's laden with *wiifm* statements.

Begin your presentation with a *wiifm* statement: "These are the objectives of my presentation. You'll find that by understanding these principles, you'll be in a better position to identify areas for improving output." This simple statement at the beginning of a presentation tells the listener what's in it for him or her to pay attention to what you have to say. After you have their attention, you can embellish the body of your presentation with benefits. Finally, at the end of the presentation, you can recap the benefits — summarize them. Doing so will help you sell your ideas and you'll be viewed as someone who considers others and their needs when suggesting ideas and action steps.

ıdnotes

1. J. E. Jones. *A "Vacuum Theory" of Assumptions.* Unpublished Paper. San Diego: Organization Universe Systems, 1989.

2. D. Walton. *Are You Communicating? You Can't Manage Without it.* New York: McGraw-Hill, Inc., 1989.

3. R.E. Lefton, V. R. Buzzotta & M. Sherberg. *Improving Productivity Through People Skills.* Cambridge: Ballinger Publishing Company, 1980.

4. V. R. Buzzotta, R. E. Lefton & M. Sherberg. *Effective Selling Through Psychology.* St. Louis: Psychological Associates, Inc., 1982.

Chapter

12

Managing Disruption and Conflict

> "If the only tool you have is a hammer,
> you tend to see every problem as a nail."
> —Abraham Maslow

> "Please find me a one-armed economist so we
> will not always hear 'on the other hand'…"
> —Herbert Hoover

Your co-worker storms into your office, livid with anger. "How could you have blown the presentation to top management?" she screams. What follows is a flurry of insults and thunder. You:
- Seethe inwardly at this unfair attack, but say nothing.
- Rail right back at her for having blown up without first getting your side of the story.
- Decide to wait until things cool down so the matter can be discussed rationally.

Surely, you have had experiences like this one. And you had to choose from among the common coping responses to conflict — anger-in, anger-out, or go to the balcony and let things vent. If you haven't, you will. Conflict is as certain as death and taxes whenever people work together.

Disruptive conflict on a team results in:
- Tension and stress.
- Anger, hard feelings, or avoidance.
- Damaged working relationships between team members.
- Distractions that keep team members from doing their jobs.

This chapter is about people getting along with others and not getting along with others and what to do about it.

Two Important Definitions

Before we begin, there are two important distinctions shown below:

Con • flict (kon' • flikt') noun.
- War, struggle, friction, combat.
- A clash of differing ideas, interests, styles, and so forth.
- *Can be disruptive — lead to low productivity, tension, and stress.*

Example:

Two people have very different work styles — one likes to carefully plan things, and the other likes to jump right into projects.

Dis • a • gree • ment (dis' • a • gre' • ment) noun.
- Differences of opinion.
- Opposing views on an issue.
- *Can be productive — lead to greater creativity.*

Example:

Two people have different ideas about how to improve quality. By discussing each idea and keeping an open mind, they discover that a combination of both is the best solution. If they don't discuss their differences, conflict may erupt.

This chapter is about conflict — the disruptive kind — and what you can do about it. There are no easy solutions — no pink pills — that work in all situations, with all people, all the time.

You will get some useful tools that work in most situations, with most people, to deal with most conflicts.

oad Map

"Imagine That" — How You Manage Conflict

When people work together, conflict is inevitable. It causes tension. It's neither fun nor productive. Play out a conflict in your imagination with a real person.

Close your eyes and imagine a long hall, as in Exhibit 12-1. No one else is in the hall. As you walk slowly toward the other end, a door opens. Out walks the person with whom you have the most conflict. This person can be anyone.

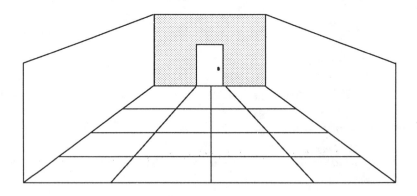

Exhibit 12-1: The Hallway

Watch what happens. Don't try to invent the situation. Just observe what happens and what you do.

How did you handle your imaginary situation?
What happened, what did you do, and what was the result? Which category below best describes your action?

Attack	Avoid	Soften	Resolve
Physically and/or verbally lash out at the other person.	Walk away from or ignore the other person.	Pretend there is no conflict and things are fine.	Get conflict out in the open and try to resolve it.

People handle conflict differently. That's because teams consist of human beings that do very human things. Sometimes they capitulate when they should stand firm, sometimes they vacillate when they should initiate, and sometimes they prefer the comfort of fellowship to the challenge of confrontation.

Model of Conflict Management Patterns

There are at least four ways to manage conflict — one that works and three that don't. Exhibit 12-2 shows the Model of Conflict Management Patterns:

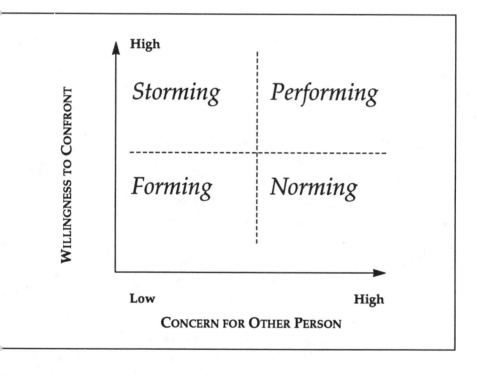

Exhibit 12-2: Conflict Management Patterns

Exhibit 12-3 shows the behaviors defining each pattern.

Storming — **Attack**
• Argues and attacks
• Puts person down
• Finds fault
• Blames
	Performing — **Resolve**
	• Acknowledges conflict
	• Tries to understand
	  both sides
	• Attempts to work
	  through/negotiate

Forming — **Avoid**
• Moves away
• Ignores
• Keeps on walking
• Says little or
  nothing
	Norming — **Soften**
	• Smoothes over conflict
	• Pretends nothing's
	  wrong
	• Gives in
	• Makes light of situation

Exhibit 12-3: Characteristics of Each Pattern

Conflict Causes — Why Conflict Happens

Effective teamwork requires successful management of disruptive conflict and the use of preventative measures to deal with it in the future. To manage conflict, you must first find what's causing it. Only then can you deal with it and prevent it from occurring again.

Think about a recent conflict situation. Why did the conflict occur? What were possible causes? Here are some examples:

Keep these points in mind when faced with conflict:
1. You can manage conflict and prevent it in the future only if:
• You know the cause(s) — why its occurring.
• You and the other person agree on the cause(s).

2. To manage conflict, do these things:
• Make sure you can describe the conflict to the other person.
• Think about what is causing the conflict, but don't assume you're right.
• Describe the conflict to the other person and get help in exploring the causes and managing it.

Conflict Situation	Possible Causes
Situation 1: Pat is a slow worker and slows down production for everyone. Someone finally blew up and told Pat to speed up or move to a different line.	• Pat may not know he's slow. • He may not be trained. • Pat may not have the right tools or equipment in working order. • He may not have the experience. • He may feel quality is more important than quantity.
Situation 2: Chris fights anything new or different. Finally, someone told her to either shape up and get with the program or ship out.	• She may think the change is not necessary. • She may not know how to make the change to a different method. • She may feel hurt that she was told (not asked) to do something new or different. • She may think her job is threatened.
Situation 3: Bill often talks behind people's backs. Finally, someone lost his cool and told Bill to mind his own business.	• Bill is concerned about something but afraid to tell the person. • Bill has been turned off by something the person did and wants to get even. • He has such a strong desire to look good that he goes so far as to make others look bad.

ᴅENT — A Four-Step Conflict-Management Process

To dent means to make an impression or effect, usually against resistance — like a dent in a car. In a team context, you'll "dent" the conflict — make an impression in it against the resistance of the other person. The good news is that it works with most people in most situations under most circumstances.

Here are the four steps:

Step 1: Describe the Conflict — First describe the conflict to the other person in a constructive, nonblaming way.

Step 2: Explore Causes — Enlist the cooperation of the other person in exploring causes.

Step 3: Negotiate a Resolution — Determine what each person must do more of, less of, or differently to deal with the conflict.

Step 4: Take Action — Implement the actions.

We'll take a closer look at each step.

Step 1: Describe the Conflict

The objective here is to introduce the conflict in a constructive way that motivates the other person to help resolve it. An "I" statement works well. Here's the formula:[1]

"I" or "I'm" + Feelings + Behavior causing the feelings + Benefits of changing the behavior or adverse consequences of not + Ask for help.

Here's an example:

Ray, I'm worried *(First person statement + Feelings)* about the delays in production on line A *(Behavior causing the feelings)*. When delays occur, orders get backlogged and customers complain *(Adverse consequences)*. Would you help me get to the bottom of this? *(Request for help)*

Try Step 1 on for size. Lynn and Tony have quite different approaches to work. Tony carefully plans things before beginning. Lynn just plunges into projects without a lot of thought or planning. The two of them were recently given the job of locating a new plant site. Tony suggested that the next several days be spent talking with the plant departments to gather information on needs for space, expansion plans, required access to railways and highways, etc. Once the specifications are nailed down, they can go to agents to see what is available.

Lynn rejected the idea. She said there's no time for gathering information. "Let's just look at what's available and we'll know when we've got the right one," she said. This caused conflict between the two of them.

You are Tony — Describe the conflict.

I'm + Feelings:

Behavior causing the feelings:

Benefits of resolving it, or negative consequences of ignoring it:

Ask for help:

Compare your approach with this one:

"I'm frustrated because we don't have a handle on the objectives, specifications, and features for the plant site. If we begin looking for a site without a plan, I'm afraid we will spend a lot of time running around without really knowing what the plant departments need and want. Can you help me with this?"

Step 2: Explore Causes
In this step you'll explore the causes of conflict and get down to the underlying issues. The objective is for both people to agree on the cause(s). First, get the other person's view, then add yours.

Try to understand the other person's position. Ask a lot of open-end questions like:
• What's your view?
• What do you see as the causes?
• What's in it for us to deal with them?
• How do you think we should deal with them?

Listen for understanding. After all, you may change your views. Even if you don't, you can't expect the other person to hear you out if you do not first hear him/her out. Following is an example of a Step 2. Notice the use of open-end probes by Tony. Using them developed a lot of give-and-take.

Lynn: "I'm really concerned about the time we have to find a site. With you it's analysis paralysis. Let's get moving on this!"

Tony: "You're concerned about not finding a site by the deadline."

Lynn: "That's right."

Tony: "What is the deadline?"

Lynn: "It's next week. It's ridiculous, that's what it is."

Tony: "You think the deadline is unrealistic?"

Lynn: "You bet I do. Those people don't know what's involved."

Tony: "I agree that the deadline is unrealistic and that the people don't know what is involved. In addition, I think they have been too vague about what they want. I don't have a clear idea about their needs. What's your reaction?"

Lynn: "You're right. We could find something we think will work and they could nix it because they don't agree on what they want."

Tony: "Then what would happen?"

Lynn: "We would be back at square one."

Tony: "Is that what you want to happen?"

Lynn: "That would be frustrating. I've got plenty of other work to do."

Tony: "Me too. What do you want to happen?"

Lynn: "I want to find a site they will buy into and get things moving."

Tony: "How do we make it happen?"

Lynn: "Let's meet with the plant manager and get his views. . ."

Step 3: Negotiate a Resolution

In this step, the parties negotiate a resolution by determining what each person must do more of, less of, or differently.

Tony: "Lynn, I appreciate your willingness to meet with the plant manager and get his views on the plant site. Who else should we include in this discussion?"

Lynn: "Here we go again. We'll have to survey the entire plant before you are satisfied."

Tony: "What if we interview the department heads? That's six people. If they are in good agreement about the specifications, we're home free. We can both talk to the plant manager and then take three department heads each. How does that sound?"

Lynn: "Okay. But we have to get moving on this. I'll agree to the surveys, if you promise we can begin looking at sites no later than tomorrow afternoon."

Tony: "You've got a deal. I'll contact the department heads and schedule the meetings for later today and tomorrow morning."

Step 4: Take Action

In this step, you'll take action. Do three things. First, put agreements in writing if appropriate. Second, commit to making them happen. Finally, set a follow-up meeting to review what was accomplished.

This process works with most conflicts in most situations with most people.

DENT Worksheet

Use this worksheet to think through how you'll manage conflict.

1. Describe the Conflict

Start with "I'm" then state your feelings. Describe the behavior causing your feelings, benefits of addressing it, or adverse impact of ignoring it. Ask for help.

(I or I'm + Feelings):

_____

_____

Behavior causing the feelings:

_____

_____

Benefits of addressing it or adverse consequences of ignoring it:

_____

_____

Ask for help:

_____

_____

2. Explore Causes

Get other person's views; listen and understand their position; then provide your views.

Questions you'll ask:

_____

_____

Views you'll present:

_____

_____

3. Negotiate a Resolution

Anticipate what you'll say below.

What I should do more of, less of, or differently:

_____

_____

What you should do more of, less of, or differently:

_____

_____

4. Take Action to Resolve the Conflict

Put in writing what action each person will take to deal with the conflict and prevent future conflicts. Set a follow-up meeting.

A word of caution. As sure as you are sitting there, there will be times when the DENT process stalls. It's those situations that we address in the next section.

When the Conflict-Management Process Stalls

We began this chapter by saying there are no pink pills for dealing with conflict. Conflict is a human relations experience where there are no rules and logic is more the exception than standard practice. When the process stalls, you have three alternatives: (a) deal with resistance; (b) take a time out; or (c) issue an ultimatum. You'll typically use these alternatives in the order listed. The ultimatum is a safety valve — to be used when all else fails.

Dealing with Resistance

Salespeople are true professionals when it comes to dealing with resistance. That's why we look to the sales literature for techniques to handle resistance. One such technique is referred to by an acronym, "APAC," for Acknowledge, Probe, Answer, and Confirm.[2]

Acknowledge the Resistance
First, acknowledge the resistance. Let the other person know you feel it is important.

Probe to Get at the Underlying Concern
Probe to fully understand the resistance from the other's perspective. Probe to get at the underlying concern or issue. Often the vocalized issue is a smoke screen, hiding the real concern.

Answer the Concern
When you fully understand the issue, answer it.

Confirm Your Answer
Do not continue the discussion until your answer is confirmed. If you don't get confirmation, repeat APAC until you do.

Here's an example:

Lynn: "You are always planning this and planning that. When do we get down to action?"

Tony: "Your concern for action is important. Tell me more."

(Acknowledge then Probe)

Lynn: "You are always wanting to plan. I'm concerned about the deadline."

Tony: "You're concerned about the deadline. What if I told you I asked for an extension and our recommendation is due on the 15th? Would you be willing to do some planning then?"

(Summarize the concern then Answer)

Lynn: "I can see some merit in surveying a few of the department heads before we look at plant sites, but not the whole plant."

Tony: "I agree. By interviewing manufacturing and engineering along with the plant manager, we should have a good feel for their objectives and specifications. So how do you feel about our meeting the deadline now?"

(Confirm)

Lynn: "Let's get started with the interviews."

Time Out — When Things Get Heated and Off-Track

When people get hostile or try to avoid talking about the conflict, you'll have to call a Time Out. You'll have to describe the barrier, roadblock, or impasse, and ask for help. Follow these two steps:
1. State the problem using "we."
2. Ask for help.

For example, "We don't seem to be getting anywhere. What shall we do?" or, "We don't see eye-to-eye on this. What do you suggest?" or, "We seem to be fighting an undeclared war. What should we do to get the discussion back on a more constructive note?"

As you see, the Time Out simply describes the problem and specifies the owners of the problem as "we." Then, there's a request for help. There is no blaming, finger pointing, or hostility. The Time Out is simply a statement of the problem both parties are having and a request for help in resolving it.

The Ultimatum

When all else fails — when Time Out stalls — then, as a last resort, use the ultimatum. It is similar to the Time Out but goes beyond. It involves three steps:

1. Describe the situation (stall) using the pronoun "we."
2. Present the options or ultimatums — "We can..."
   - Do nothing.
   - Keep trying to resolve the problem.
   - Take a break — try again later.
   - Call the boss or someone else to help resolve this.
3. Give the other person the choice — "What's your preference?"

Role Negotiation — The Pinch-Crunch Model

Role negotiation is a process described by John Sherwood and John Glidewell to illustrate how team relationships are established and roles negotiated so team members can get down to the business at hand.[3] When a new team comes together or an existing team embarks on a new initiative it is imperative that two sets of roles and expectations be negotiated:

- Task roles — what each team member will contribute to the goal or project.
- Relationship expectations — how the team members will work together.

The Pinch-Crunch Model, illustrated in Exhibit 12-4, shows how change can enter the equation leading to either constructive or destructive consequences. The model is cyclical and includes four phases:

- Phase 1: Negotiating Roles and Expectations
- Phase 2: Stability
- Phase 3: Productivity
- Phase 4: Pinch-Crunch (Disruption).

Phase 1: Negotiating Roles and Expectations
When people enter a relationship, it is essential to negotiate roles and expectations by openly discussing what needs to be done by whom and how they'll work together. If this process is successful, working agreements are reached and roles are clear. If it is ignored, then assumptions are made by each team member about who will do what and how they'll collectively operate as a team.

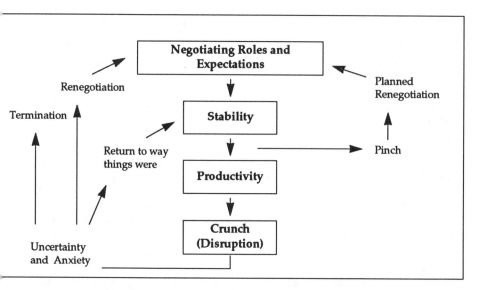

Exhibit 12-4: Pinch-Crunch Model

Phase 2: Stability

As sufficient information is exchanged, assumptions are openly discussed and the team members become comfortable with the level of certainty about the others. The relationship stabilizes.

Uncertainty is reduced to an acceptable level and those involved are satisfied with the predictability of their task expectations and how they're working together toward common goals. Roles are clearly defined and each person knows what is expected and what to expect of others.

The level of stability in the relationship is a direct function of each member's comfort with two things: (a) expectations of individual members are being met; and (b) each person is fulfilling his/her role.

Phase 3: Productivity

With this level of comfort and predictability, the team can get down to the business at hand — working together toward the goals they thought were possible and that served as the basis for organizing the team in the first place.

Consider, for example, a basketball team. Initially, the five players walked onto the practice floor wondering: What's my role? What's the role of others? How will we work together to become a first-class team? How is this coach going to operate?

Later, after a lot of coaching and many practice sessions and games, realistic goals crystallize along with roles and coordination requirements for executing the repertoire of plays.

There is now stability, predictability, and shared expectations — all the essential ingredients for a mature and productive relationship.

Ideally, energy focuses on achieving synergy — the synergistic team achieves results that are greater than the sum of the individual contributions of the members, like winning the basketball championship.

There's no guarantee that the team will become productive and synergistic, but at least the energy of the parties is diverted away from attempting to understand and be understood, making assumptions, and evaluating performance of one another against implicit or explicit expectations. The parties can now get down to the business at hand.

Stability and commitment to shared expectations governs behaviors and fosters productivity for a period of time. Teams may be productive for days, weeks, or months. But inevitably, and usually without warning — pinch and crunch — disruption occurs.

Phase 4: Pinch-Crunch (Disruption)
Disruption occurs because there is a violation of expectations — either those explicitly agreed to, or assumed — or, there's an external intrusion into the system.

Disruption occurs because: (a) critical information is not fully disclosed in the earlier phases, and/or (b) people change as a result of their environment. In other words, this disruption may be external or internal.

External Disruption
External disruption occurs when a new person is assigned to a work team, when there are changes to work policies and procedures, when there are reorganizations or budget cuts, and the like. All these things can disrupt stability by creating new expectations or violating existing ones.

For example, a work team communicating openly, unselfishly sharing resources, and mutually supporting one another is disrupted by the introduction of a bonus plan tied to individual achievement. As a result, people withhold information that's critical and may even attempt to sabotage the efforts of their team mates.

Internal Disruption

Internal disruption occurs simply with the disclosure of previously withheld information, or with natural changes in people as they gain new experiences, interests, insights, and skills.

When a changed person returns to an unchanged role, then expectations are no longer being met. That's when conflict occurs and coping mechanisms either reduce or fuel the conflict.

For example, if the relationship is open and constructive and based on a firm foundation of clarifying expectations, validating assumptions, and communication, conflict resolution may be easy.

If the relationship is built precipitously on untested assumptions, limited communication, and infrequent or imbalanced feedback, then resolving the conflict may be emotionally trying, inefficient, and painful.

Pinch

Change is inevitable — the only constant in our world. Small changes are easy to deal with. Other changes are more difficult. Changes eventually lead to a pinch — a small problem or disturbance between team members. Whenever there's a pinch, it's a signal of impending disruption and raises the possibility of a renegotiation. Renegotiation is easier at this point since the team is not under a crisis, yet.

Crunch

Without renegotiation, there is increasing frequency and intensity of disruption which causes uncertainty and anxiety. A disruption and the anxiety that ensues is managed two ways: (1) as a new source of information and an opportunity to adjust expectations and renegotiate roles; or, (2) as a source of great tension that stimulates an urgency to return to the way things were. It's paradoxical, though, that when the team is most open to change —

when there's a crunch — strong inhibiting forces create anxiety and a desire to quickly return to the way things were. Unfortunately, this is a short-term solution since the underlying cause of the crunch is never dealt with.

Lessons from the Pinch-Crunch Model

There are several very important lessons to be learned from the Pinch-Crunch Model. They are:

1. *Negotiate expectations and roles when a new team is formed or when a new initiative is undertaken by the team.* This clarifies who will do what and how the team will operate. It provides the basis for stability and productivity.

2. *Don't make assumptions and act on them as if they were true.* As suggested in the last chapter, if you make assumptions (and we all do), check them out. Open up communication channels and find out which assumptions are valid and which are not.

3. *Be vigilant for pinches.* Whenever there's stress and tension on a team, the stability and productivity is threatened. It's a signal for planned renegotiation of expectations and roles. If this does not occur, the pinch will most certainly become a crunch.

4. *Acknowledge there's a crunch, and the system (team) is open for change.* Anxiety and uncertainty are the stimuli. Avoid the tendency to return to the way things were — ignoring the real problem that caused the crunch in the first place. Rather, initiate role and expectation renegotiation.

5. *Termination of the relationship is always an alternative.* Examine the positive and negative consequences of terminating the relationship and do what appears most constructive and logical for the team.

Endnotes

1. R. E. Lefton, V. R. Buzzotta & M. Sherberg. *Improving Productivity Through People Skills*. Cambridge: Ballinger, 1980.

2. V. R. Buzzotta, R. E. Lefton & M. Sherberg. *Effective Selling Through Psychology*. St. Louis: Psychological Associates, 1982.

3. J. J. Sherwood and J. C. Glidewell. "Planned Renegotiation: A Norm-Setting OD Intervention." *Annual Handbook for Group Facilitators*, San Diego: University Associates, 1973.

PART THREE

**Tools of
the Trade**

Chapter

13RTEEN

Planning Future Opportunities

"Business is like a war in one respect,
if its grand strategy is correct, any number
of tactical errors can be made and yet the
enterprise proves successful."
    —*General Robert E. Wood*
        former President of Sears

I **I** t's tough getting these product managers to think strategically," Adams asserted. "I know," Stewart replied. "I think it's because we've been through so many difficult years and they were told they either lived or died by the quarterly success of their products."

Adams remained silent, staring at the papers strewn across the table but seeing nothing. Then he asked, "Is the problem that they don't know how to think strategically, or does pressure for results inhibit their thinking?" "Probably both," Stewart answered quickly.

This scenario illustrates the tough balancing act of many people in business. Short-term profitability is important — as is cash flow. But if the long-term strategic well-being of a business unit is to be preserved, management must go beyond the quarter-by-quarter outlook.

Why do some business units thrive and flourish while others accomplish less and grow slower than they might? One answer is that those units that prosper look to the future to plan change, establish sound strategy, and carefully chart their destinies.

They regularly ask key strategic questions like:[1]
1. Where are we now?
2. If no radical changes are made, where will we be in one year, two years, three years?
3. Is this acceptable? If not, what specific strategies must we employ to get us where we want to be? What must we do to achieve our mission?

This chapter is about examining where you are and where you want to go. It's about determining priorities for allocating resources to productively achieve short-term objectives while vigorously pursuing strategic opportunities.

This chapter addresses strategic planning as a broad organizational process, then focuses more specifically on product/service positioning strategies and identifying opportunities to become more customer focused. Planning will help you focus your resources on those areas that have the greatest payoff for your business unit or team.

The tools and techniques presented in this chapter will help you and your team grapple with tough questions about where you want to focus your efforts and resources. Doing so will help identify the right levers to pull in the right ways to close the gap between the situation as it is and what it can ideally become.

Road Map

Planning Defined

Lest things get confused, here are some definitions that differentiate some commonly confused terms and methods used in planning.

Strategic and Tactical Planning
Strategic planning is the process of determining the major objectives and courses of action (strategies) the organization will pursue and how resources will be allocated to achieve the objectives in an optimally productive and efficient way.

Tactical planning takes broad strategies and translates them into specific objectives and action plans for a subcomponent of the organization like Research and Development.

Different Approaches to Long-Range Planning
In this chapter we'll focus on strategic planning. More specifically, we'll address three alternatives for team planning:
1. *Strategic Planning* — Formulating general strategy for exploiting opportunities and avoiding threats. You'll use this method to develop general strategy, particularly if your business is more profit focused than product/service or customer focused.
2. *Product/Service Planning* — Planning to determine future product/service emphasis in each market segment and the appropriate strategies for maintaining, developing, exploring, or phasing down products/services. This method is useful for developing and maintaining product and service focus.
3. *Planning Customer-Focus Strategies* — Identifying changing customer needs and strategies to meet those needs better than the competition. This is a useful approach for developing and maintaining customer focus.

Behavior Model of Team Planning Patterns

The Model of Team Planning Patterns consists of two factors:
1. Clarity and relevance of the plan
2. Involvement and commitment to executing it

Clarity and Relevance of Plan

An effective plan is both clear and relevant. It is clear if it provides specific direction. People can use it to determine priorities — what's important and what's not. A plan is relevant if it considers issues like the mission, internal strengths and weaknesses, and external opportunities and barriers.

To be relevant a team plan must support a higher-level mission or plan, of which the team is a part. The higher-level plan can be from the department, division, corporation, or other component of the organization.

Involvement and Commitment

Effective strategic plans are established in a way that involves all team members. When everyone on a team contributes to the plan, team members share the same understanding and high level of commitment.

The Model of Team Planning Patterns (Exhibit 13-1) shows how a team's strategic plan consists of both clarity and relevance and the involvement and commitment of team members that must execute it.

Following are examples of how team members describe each pattern:

- *Forming:* We don't have a plan, or it's so general and vague it doesn't provide much direction for the team.
- *Storming:* Our plan is specific, relevant, and clear but it was mandated — handed to us with little input. As a result, commitment to executing it is low.
- *Norming:* We were all actively involved in developing our strategic plan, but it is so general and broad almost anything we do seems consistent with it.
- *Performing:* There's a lot of commitment to our strategic plan, which presents specific and challenging objectives and courses of action for the future.

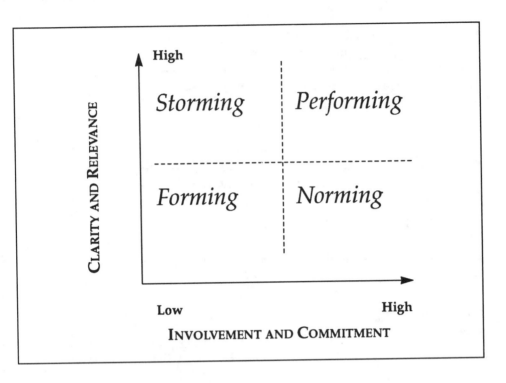

Exhibit 13-1: Team Planning Patterns

Strategic Planning

Exhibit 13-2 shows a strategic planning framework. Notice the arrows showing the relationship between mission, organization, and external environment. This illustrates that none of the elements is considered to be in a vacuum — each must be considered in full view of all others.

Within the organization, you must assess strengths and weaknesses of your products or services, people, structure, delivery system, and the like. Similarly, you must identify opportunities and threats on the horizon in your external environment. Both analyses must be done in view of the mission — what business or businesses you want to be in, your markets and customers, and your values.

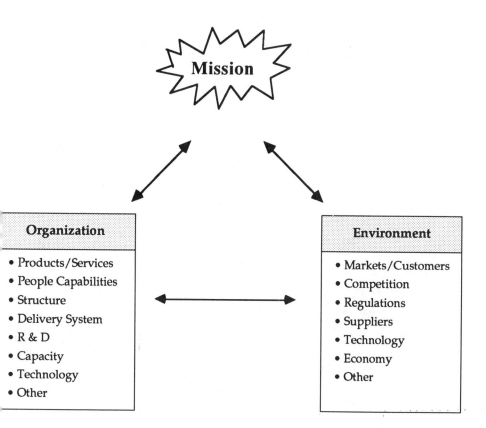

Mission

Organization

- Products/Services
- People Capabilities
- Structure
- Delivery System
- R & D
- Capacity
- Technology
- Other

Environment

- Markets/Customers
- Competition
- Regulations
- Suppliers
- Technology
- Economy
- Other

xhibit 13-2: Strategic Planning Framework

Once the team identifies strengths, weaknesses, opportunities and threats, you can assemble a matrix like that shown in Exhibit 13-3. This matrix provides several insights for the team. For example, where the team's strengths are positioned to capitalize on an opportunity, the team develops a strategy to *exploit the opportunity*. Unless the unit's strengths must be used to avoid a threat — then the strategy is to address the threat without unduly *draining resources*. Thus, for the strengths, the team must decide how to best *allocate its resources* to exploit opportunities and avoid threats.

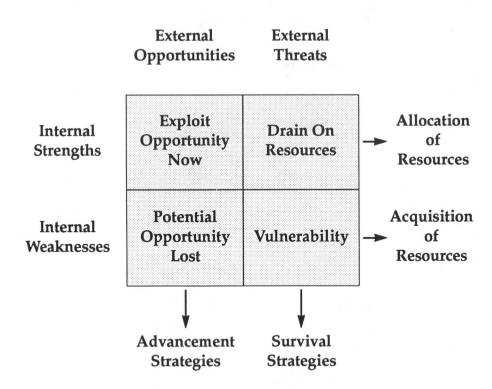

Exhibit 13-3: SWOT Matrix

The team looks at its weaknesses in a similar way. Where there's a weakness preventing the team from capitalizing on an opportunity, you have the predicament of a potential *opportunity lost*. Worst case, where there's a threat that threatens a team's weakness, the team is *vulnerable*. Weaknesses must be dealt with by *acquiring resources* to bolster the unit so it avoids *vulnerabilities* and lost *opportunities*.

The team's general *advancement strategies* are those where it uses its resources to pursue opportunities. *Survival strategies* reflect how the team chooses to address threats in the environment.

As this process illustrates, planning is a matter of deciding how to focus resources. And the term "focus" is important. If you do not focus your resources on exploiting a few key opportunities and avoiding major threats, you'll quickly diffuse creativity and energy.

Team Involvement in Strategic Planning

Strategic planning is speculative. No one knows what the future will bring. Therefore, teams have to rely on hunches about the external environment. Then, as the future becomes the present, the team continually evaluates the results of implemented strategies and tests assumptions against reality. On the basis of this new information, strategies are formulated and plans are adjusted for future opportunities.

It's important for all team members to be actively involved in strategic planning. It's likely that each person has an important piece of the puzzle — a perspective that adds useful insight. Here's a procedure for maximizing team involvement in strategic planning.

Step 1: Individual Identification of Strengths, Weaknesses, Opportunities, and Threats

Individually, team members think through strengths and weaknesses of the organization and opportunities and threats in the environment. The framework and items in Exhibit 13-2 (page 221) can serve as thought triggers. Or, use the Strategic Planning Survey at the end of the chapter.

When possible, gather information available from industry groups, trade journals, and the popular press. Many of these sources have strong research staffs that investigate trends and make data-based projections about the future. This information may add insight to or validate your thinking.

Step 2: Individual Sharing of Strengths

Begin with internal strengths. In a round-robin fashion, each team member reports a strength and why he/she feels it's a strength. A recorder lists the strengths on a flip chart. Continue until all strengths are listed. A ground rule here is that there should be no value judgments. Just list strengths on the flip chart.

Step 3: Consensus on Major Strengths

After all strengths are listed, the team should discuss them. Look for ways to combine or group the strengths. Then, using a consensus process like that described in Chapter 10, decide on the most important strengths. Most teams will define 5 to 15.

Step 4: Repeat Steps 2 and 3 for
Weaknesses, Opportunities, and Threats
This same process of reporting, flip charting, discussing, and reaching consensus should occur for weaknesses, opportunities, and threats.

Step 5: Prepare a SWOT Matrix
Use the SWOT data to prepare a matrix like the one following. This might be a good time to take a break from the planning and assign each individual the analytical tasks of considering each cell and the strategies that make most sense. A strategy makes sense if it appears logical — if the underlying assumptions (about strengths, weaknesses, opportunities, and threats) seem valid and the potential payoffs seem reasonable given the investment of the team's resources.

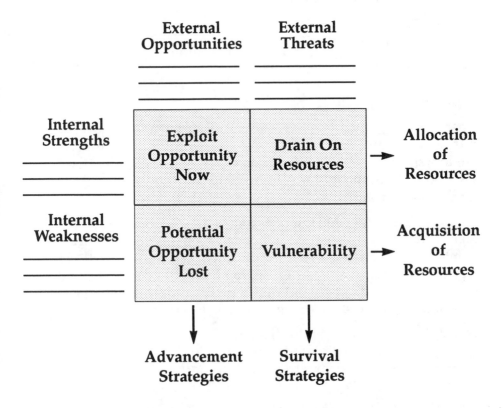

Step 6: Reach Consensus on Strategies

Use a consensus process to reach agreement on the strategies the team will pursue. Or, use a decision-making process like that defined in Chapter 9 to decide from among the alternatives.

Step 7: Develop a Communication and Implementation Plan

Devise an action plan for communicating the strategies to the appropriate people and a tactical plan for organizing and allocating resources. The tactical plan should include time lines and accountabilities for execution.

Step 8: Establish a Monitoring System

Set up a system for closely monitoring the environment to see if the assumptions you made about the future become reality. Also, monitor the results of implemented actions to determine if the outcomes expected are achieved. Make adjustments in strategies and action plans as needed to address unanticipated environmental events and to produce the results expected.

Product/Service-Driven Planning

Business units that are product- or service-driven have numerous opportunities for growth shown in Exhibit 13-4.[3] They are:
- Deeper penetration of current markets with current or modified products/services (*Cells 1 and 2*).
- Expansion into new markets with current or modified products/services (*Cells 4 and 5*).
- New product/service development for current markets (*Cell 3*).
- New product/service development for new markets (*Cell 6*).

Current products/services are those now being produced and delivered.

Modified products/services have improved features and functions offering unique advantages and benefits.

New products/services fill a new need.

Current markets and geographic areas are clearly defined in terms of their characteristics and customers.

New market segments define new geographic areas with clearly different customers.

Products/Services

		Current	Modified	New
Markets	**Current**	1	2	3
	New	4	5	6

Exhibit 13-4: Product/Markets Matrix

Strategy Development
Exhibit 13-5 shows strategies for capitalizing on opportunities in each of the six cells. A business unit obviously cannot pursue all the opportunities for business development. The team must conduct an analysis for each cell by making assumptions about market size, competition, growth of market, opportunities/barriers to entry, buying motives, and product/service strengths and weaknesses. The team SWOT analysis helps determine the most realistic priorities to pursue based upon assumptions about threats and opportunities and assessment of strengths and weaknesses.

If you have multiple products with multiple markets, this process becomes more complex. For simplicity, we have included a two by three matrix (Exhibit 13-5). The size of the matrix and the number of cells depend on the number of products/services and markets you have currently and are willing to consider.

Products/Services

	Current	Modified	New
Current	• Optimize sale of current products in current markets	• Modify current products to differentiate and add value	• Explore needs in current markets and develop new products
New	• Identify new markets for current products	• Modify existing products to meet needs in new markets	• Acquire or develop new products for new markets

Markets (label at left, spanning Current/New rows)

Exhibit 13-5: Product/Service-Driven Strategies

Product Planning Process

Exhibit 13-6 shows a partially completed future opportunity matrix for a company that provides health care and beauty products.

Here are the procedures for evaluating each cell:

1. Classify Products/Services and Markets

Given the mission of the unit and other considerations, determine the best way to develop the products/markets matrix.

2. Determine the Applicability of Each Cell

Some products/services do not make sense for some markets. For example, department stores generally do not carry vitamins. Put an N/A in each cell for "not applicable."

3. Decide on Future Emphasis

Individually, the team members should decide on the future emphasis in each cell. Options include: Develop (D), Maintain (M), Explore (E), or Phase down (P).

4. Discuss Assumptions for High-Priority Areas

Individually, each team member should list the assumptions made for each future emphasis decision including: size of market, competition, market growth, buying motives and behavior, position in market, product strengths and weaknesses, and the like.

	Products					
	Current			New		
	Hand Lotion	Perfume/ Cologne	Lip Stick	Vitamins	After Shave	Face Cream
Current Markets — *Drug Stores*	M	M	M	E	D	D
Department Stores	M	M	M	N/A	E	E
New Markets — *Supermarkets*	D	D	D	E	E	E
Catalog/ Direct Mail	E	E	E	E	E	E

Exhibit 13-6: Product/Markets Matrix

5. Reach Team Consensus

Each team member reports the decision for the first cell. The Ds, Ms, and Ps are listed on a flip chart. Each team member supports the decision with the assumptions made. After discussing the decision and assumptions, the team reaches consensus on the decision on future emphasis. This is repeated for all cells.

A variation of this step is to use the decision-making process presented in an earlier chapter. After individually thinking through the matrix, the "must-have" and "desirable objectives" should be clear in your own mind. Write them down. This step is completed for all products/services in all markets using the decision-making process presented earlier.

6. Determine Product Positioning Requirements

The team should discuss and list on a flip chart the product positioning requirements for the high-priority future emphasis products/services and markets. This includes features and benefits, technology, service requirements, pricing, packaging, promotion, distribution, and the like. It is important that the positioning requirements be made in full view of competitive products/services. The question is this: "What is required to meet the needs and do so better than the competition?"

7. Determine Resource Requirements

Next, the team must determine the resources required including R&D, Manufacturing, Marketing, Distribution, Sales, Information Systems, etc.

8. Tactical Planning

Put together a tactical plan that spells out how the resources are coordinated to meet the objectives for quality, quantity, cost, and time lines. This action plan should also include who'll finalize the plan and who you'll present your plan to for approval.

Product/Service Positioning Requirements

Once a product or service strategy is in place, the next step is to identify the specific positioning requirements. The following questions are helpful in providing insight about what must be done:[4]

- What product features, advantages, and benefits are required?
- What characteristics will be used to differentiate the product or service in the marketplace?
- What technological support will be needed?
- What are the requirements for packaging?
- What are the delivery requirements?
- What will be required for ongoing service?
- What are the marketing and promotional needs?
- How will the product/service be priced?
- When will the product/service be launched?

Team Capabilities Requirements

The next question is what capabilities will be required to successfully position the product/service in the marketplace. Here are some helpful questions about capabilities:[5]
- What R & D capabilities will we need?
- What special technology will be required?
- What production, manufacturing, operations capabilities and capacities will be needed?
- What marketing capability and intelligence is desired?
- What sales methods, skills, approaches, and people will be required?
- What are the various distribution methods and how do they compare from a cost-benefit standpoint?
- What level of capitalization is desired and what financing will be required?
- How will we source and manage raw materials?

Planning Customer-Focused Strategies

Teams that are primarily customer-focused will continually develop strategies for continuously enhancing customer responsiveness and satisfaction. These teams compete by forming long-term partnerships with their customers. They continually respond to current needs by adding value. They respond to emerging needs with continuous product or service innovations.

The strategies you'll formulate include:
- Providing alternatives for current customer needs.
- Developing new products/services to fill new and emerging needs of current customers.

But first, you need an established, long-term relationship with customers — a relationship built on trust where the supplier has in-depth knowledge of the customer's business and long-term plans. Tom Peters provides sage advice on creating total customer responsiveness in his seminal work, *Thriving on Chaos*.[6] He offers these prescriptions:

Prescription 1: Specialize —
Create Niches and Differentiate

Rather than thinking about sharing markets, business units need to think about creating market niches. Market sharing strategies often focus on getting more of the pie through pricing, promotion, advertising, and distribution. Creating a bigger pie or a new pie — a niche — requires specializing in a product or service area and focusing on:

- Changing rapidly in response to changing customer needs.
- Continually adding value and differentiating in the niche by offering distinctive features and services that customers want.
- Creating new ideas and product/service innovations at least at the rate of one every 90 days — individually the differentiators may be mundane but collectively they may be awesome.

Here's how. . .

Gather Information

Identify a slumbering product or service. Meet with end-user customers, people in the distribution channel, suppliers, and employees at all levels and functions of the organization. Ask the question: How can we add value and differentiate this product or service in the market niche?

Assess

Do a cost benefit analysis. Is the investment in adding value and differentiating likely to broaden the niche and add sales?

Execute

Relaunch the product or service as quickly as possible, highlighting the value added and differentiating characteristics.

Follow up

Do a differentiation assessment regularly. Is the differentiating strategy working? What can we do more of or differently to add value and differentiate?

Prescription 2: Provide Top
Quality as Perceived by the Customer

Regarding quality, Tom Peters makes four important points: (1) customers will pay a lot for quality; (2) firms that provide top quality prosper; (3) continuous pursuit of top-quality products and services invigorates employees at all levels; and (4) no company ever has a safe lead in quality since new entrants into the market are continually defining new possibilities for the customer.

Here's how to mount a quality revolution:

Define quality in customer terms
Don't make assumptions about customer perceptions of quality. Ask the customer. Define quality specifically and in customer terms.

Deliver quality
Never compromise quality or walk past a quality problem. Take decisive action, almost regardless of cost, to deliver the highest quality.

Measure and Improve
Collect data about quality — internally and from customers. Continually find ways to make quality enhancements. Become obsessed with continuous improvement.

Prescription 3: Provide Exceptional Service,
Emphasizing the Intangibles

The intangibles — service and customer responsiveness — are a distinct and difficult-to-copy competitive advantage. Emphasize the intangibles like reliability and service. Under promise and over deliver. Always keep this formula foremost in your mind:

$$CP = \frac{D}{E}$$

Customer Perceptions (CP) equals Delivery (D) divided by Expectations (E)

Here's how to continually maximize customer perceptions:

Create a Total Product or Service Concept
Take a generic product or service and augment it with intangibles like friendly service, quick response, 24-hour delivery, drop shipping, and the like.

Get Customer Reactions
Invite customers to compare the total product or service concept to what they have now and what they can get from the competition. Probe for new possibilities.

Continually Seek Ways to Provide Superior Service
Encourage and solicit ideas for adding intangibles to the product concept — to exceed customer expectations.

Get Closer and Closer to the Customer
Identify ways to get closer to the customer (end users or people in the distribution channels) to provide an ongoing source of information about competitive activity, changing customer needs, and product or service perceptions.

Prescription 4: Turn Manufacturing Into a Marketing Weapon

End the practice of single-mindedly pursing means to lower labor costs. Instead, elevate manufacturing as a marketing tool. Since quality, responsiveness, speed, flexibility, and innovativeness are all controlled by operations or manufacturing, determine ways to make them more customer responsive and quality conscious. If manufacturing can add value and make something a little better each day, you'll reduce cycle time and increase competitiveness.

Here's how. . .

Identify Critical Result Areas
Identify the critical business results — things the business unit must do exceptionally well to add value and differentiate in the market place. Examples include product research, development and manufacturing, order fulfillment, and the like.

Define Horizontal Processes
Define the horizontal processes that must be linked if the unit is to achieve the critical result area.

Organize Around Process not Just Function

Functional barriers often get in the way of or dilute the effectiveness of the organization to execute core business processes and achieve critical results areas. When possible, break down functional barriers and organize around processes.

Strategic Planning Survey — Analysis of Opportunities and Threats

Directions: Consider the external environment. Rate your agreement with each statement by circling the response that best reflects your views. List the priority opportunities and threats for the next 12 to 18 months.

Our Markets					
1. Our current markets provide a lot of opportunity for future growth.	Strongly Disagree	Disagree	Agree more than Disagree	Agree	Strongly Agree
2. We have identified many good ideas for new products and services for our current market segments.	Strongly Disagree	Disagree	Agree more than Disagree	Agree	Strongly Agree
3. We have identified a number of new product or service opportunities to evaluate or enter in the future.	Strongly Disagree	Disagree	Agree more than Disagree	Agree	Strongly Agree
4. We have adequate programs underway to capitalize on new product or service ideas.	Strongly Disagree	Disagree	Agree more than Disagree	Agree	Strongly Agree

Our Competitors					
5. We know our competition and their strengths and weaknesses.	Strongly Disagree	Disagree	Agree more than Disagree	Agree	Strongly Agree
6. We are aware of the critical competitive advantages that we must maintain over our competitors.	Strongly Disagree	Disagree	Agree more than Disagree	Agree	Strongly Agree
7. Our competitive advantages will be difficult for our competitors to duplicate or equal in the next few years.	Strongly Disagree	Disagree	Agree more than Disagree	Agree	Strongly Agree
8. Competition from other organizations will not increase significantly in the next several years.	Strongly Disagree	Disagree	Agree more than Disagree	Agree	Strongly Agree

Our Customers

9.	We have clearly defined our target customers.	Strongly Disagree	Disagree	Agree more than Disagree	Agree	Strongly Agree
10.	We are able to satisfy our customers' needs better than the competition.	Strongly Disagree	Disagree	Agree more than Disagree	Agree	Strongly Agree
11.	We have a strong image and customer loyalty in our markets.	Strongly Disagree	Disagree	Agree more than Disagree	Agree	Strongly Agree
12.	Our current customer base will grow rather than decline in the next several years.	Strongly Disagree	Disagree	Agree more than Disagree	Agree	Strongly Agree

Other Opportunities or Threats

13.	Government regulations will have little effect on our business in the next year or so.	Strongly Disagree	Disagree	Agree more than Disagree	Agree	Strongly Agree
14.	Changes in demographics (e.g., population growth by age group or region) will impact our business favorably.	Strongly Disagree	Disagree	Agree more than Disagree	Agree	Strongly Agree
15.	Social changes within our market (e.g., double-income families, household computers) will positively impact our business.	Strongly Disagree	Disagree	Agree more than Disagree	Agree	Strongly Agree
16.	Economic factors (e.g., interest rates, inflation, employment) will affect us positively over the next few years.	Strongly Disagree	Disagree	Agree more than Disagree	Agree	Strongly Agree
17.	Technological advances (e.g., information technologies) will positively affect our business operations in the future.	Strongly Disagree	Disagree	Agree more than Disagree	Agree	Strongly Agree
18.	The local or national political climate will have little impact on our business over the next few years.	Strongly Disagree	Disagree	Agree more than Disagree	Agree	Strongly Agree
19.	We can rely on our external resources — other companies, suppliers, vendors — to consistently provide us with the products and services we need.	Strongly Disagree	Disagree	Agree more than Disagree	Agree	Strongly Agree
20.	We actively seek many external means of growth such as partnerships, joint ventures, acquisitions.	Strongly Disagree	Disagree	Agree more than Disagree	Agree	Strongly Agree

What do you see as the 1 or 2 most important *Opportunities* to consider in planning?

_____

_____

_____

_____

What do you see as the 1 or 2 most important *Threats* to consider in planning?

_____

_____

_____

_____

Strategic Planning Survey — Analysis of Strengths and Weaknesses

Directions: Consider the internal organization environment. Rate your agreement with each statement by circling the response that best reflects your views. List what you believe to be the greatest strengths and the greatest weaknesses to consider in planning.

Our People

1.	We have strong depth and breadth of management talent in the company.	Strongly Disagree	Disagree	Agree more than Disagree	Agree	Strongly Agree
2.	We have technically competent, responsive, and service-oriented personnel who serve our customers.	Strongly Disagree	Disagree	Agree more than Disagree	Agree	Strongly Agree
3.	Our operations, manufacturing, and other support functions provide high-quality, responsive service to the people who serve our customers.	Strongly Disagree	Disagree	Agree more than Disagree	Agree	Strongly Agree
4.	We have a good mix of visionary, futurist thinkers and planners and day-to-day, tactical doers.	Strongly Disagree	Disagree	Agree more than Disagree	Agree	Strongly Agree

Our Organization Structure and Management Systems

5.	We are effectively structured and organized to promote effective communication, support and teamwork.	Strongly Disagree	Disagree	Agree more than Disagree	Agree	Strongly Agree
6.	We have well-developed management systems for planning, goal setting, performance review, and tying pay to performance.	Strongly Disagree	Disagree	Agree more than Disagree	Agree	Strongly Agree
7.	Our information systems provide timely, thorough, and accurate information about our business and customers.	Strongly Disagree	Disagree	Agree more than Disagree	Agree	Strongly Agree
8.	We monitor the performance of our business, products and services, and subsidiaries and take timely action to correct variances from plan.	Strongly Disagree	Disagree	Agree more than Disagree	Agree	Strongly Agree

Our Products/Services/Delivery System

9.	We have a strong delivery system that enables us to fully penetrate our markets.	Strongly Disagree	Disagree	Agree more than Disagree	Agree	Strongly Agree
10.	Our advertising/public relations activities are effective in promoting our products and services and enhancing our image.	Strongly Disagree	Disagree	Agree more than Disagree	Agree	Strongly Agree
11.	We provide a full range of products and services to meet our customers' needs.	Strongly Disagree	Disagree	Agree more than Disagree	Agree	Strongly Agree
12.	We have effective capabilities for originating and developing new products and services responsive to customers' needs	Strongly Disagree	Disagree	Agree more than Disagree	Agree	Strongly Agree

Our Financial Situation

13.	We do not foresee significant problems related to cash flow or finances over the next few years.	Strongly Disagree	Disagree	Agree more than Disagree	Agree	Strongly Agree
14.	We set realistic sales and profit objectives and usually meet them.	Strongly Disagree	Disagree	Agree more than Disagree	Agree	Strongly Agree
15.	We have reasonably accurate sales, cash flow, and profit information available.	Strongly Disagree	Disagree	Agree more than Disagree	Agree	Strongly Agree
16.	We have ready access to debt and/or equity to permit healthy growth and fund our plans for expanding the business.	Strongly Disagree	Disagree	Agree more than Disagree	Agree	Strongly Agree

Our Climate and Culture

17.	We have a very strong orientation to quality and customer service.	Strongly Disagree	Disagree	Agree more than Disagree	Agree	Strongly Agree
18.	We are very results oriented and excellent in our execution.	Strongly Disagree	Disagree	Agree more than Disagree	Agree	Strongly Agree
19.	We are very innovative and open to change.	Strongly Disagree	Disagree	Agree more than Disagree	Agree	Strongly Agree
20.	We anticipate the future and set the current situation in motion in a very planful and proactive way.	Strongly Disagree	Disagree	Agree more than Disagree	Agree	Strongly Agree

What do you see as the 1 or 2 most important *Strengths* to consider in planning?

_____

_____

_____

_____

What do you see as the 1 or 2 most important *Weaknesses* to consider in planning?

_____

_____

_____

_____

Strategic Planning Survey —
Priorities for the Next 12 to 18 Months

Directions: Considering the environmental opportunities and threats, and the organizational strengths and weaknesses, what do you see as the two major priorities for the next 12 to 18 months? That is, what should be your direction, strategy, and objectives over the next 12 to 18 months? Please list them below.

Priority 1:

_____

_____

_____

_____

Priority 2:

_____

_____

_____

_____

ndnotes

1. T. L. Whelan & J. D. Hunger. *Strategic Management*. Menlo Park: Addison Wesley, 1984.

2. B. B. Tregoe, J. W. Zimmerman, R. A. Smith, and P. M. Tobia. *Vision in Action*. New York: Simon & Schuster, 1989.

3. B. B. Tregoe, J. W. Zimmerman, R. A. Smith, and P. M. Tobia. *Vision in Action*. New York: Simon & Schuster, 1989.

4. B. B. Tregoe, J. W. Zimmerman, R. A. Smith, and P. M. Tobia. *Vision in Action*. New York: Simon & Schuster, 1989.

5. Tom Peters. *Thriving on Chaos: Handbook for a Management Revolution*. New York: Alfred A Knopf, 1987.

Chapter

14

Appraising Team Performance

*"An individual without information cannot
take responsibility; an individual who is given
information cannot help but take responsibility."*
> —*Jan Carlzon, President*
> *Scandinavian Airlines*

▰▰▐ wish my manager would go over step-by-step the details on my appraisal so I could find out the areas he used to judge me. I really had no idea how he came to the conclusion that he had, except at the end I was told I did a fine job. But what areas did he use?" [1]

If this scenario sounds familiar, you certainly are not alone. Inarguably, performance appraisal is the most powerful and least expensive tool for directing, managing, motivating, and developing the performance and potential of teams and individuals. That probably explains why formal performance appraisals are conducted in 94% of U. S. companies.[2] But many people view performance reviews with the same lack of enthusiasm as IRS forms. So what's the problem?

Most problems with performance appraisal can be traced to the tool itself or the way it's used. In this chapter we'll address how to overcome both problems and develop a tool and a process that works — one that helps continuously develop team performance and the potential of each of the team members to assume more responsibility.

A properly developed appraisal process can serve as a contract between the team members and the team. It informs people about what's expected and how performance will be appraised.

During the appraisal period, an effective appraisal tool and process can help determine what the team members must start doing, continue doing, or stop doing to be more effective. This serves an important developmental function that may suggest training to improve the ability to perform.

But suppose a team member has the skills to do the job but is still not performing. The issue is likely motivation — or lack of motivation. Since the elements of an effective motivation strategy include *feedback, goal setting, team problem solving*, and *incentives*, performance appraisal is the tool to ensure these elements fully motivate the team members.

For example, *feedback* given periodically helps ensure that the team member knows how he or she is doing. *Goals* are set that specify what the team member should be doing. The team participates in *problem-solving* barriers that impede productivity. Finally, decisions about how to equitably allocate *incentives* are made contingent on a fair appraisal of performance.[3]

By using the techniques and applying the skills in this chapter, you and your team can construct a meaningful appraisal tool and use a process that serves the purposes you want — purposes like clarifying expected performance, focusing teamwork, reviewing progress, and developing performance. And the team can use the tool for continuous improvement of performance and development of potential to perform more complex tasks. All this means better job results.

Road Map

Purposes of Team Appraisal

There are numerous purposes of performance appraisal. They include:[4]

- Ensuring mutual understanding of performance expectations.
- Building confidence between manager and direct reports.
- Clarifying misunderstanding regarding performance expectations.
- Identifying training and development needs.
- Supporting decisions about pay and bonuses.
- Early identification of potential for promotion.
- Sustaining and enhancing motivation.
- Fostering communication and feedback.
- Ongoing management of performance by setting expectations, periodically reviewing progress, and conducting the overall evaluation.

Over 30 percent of companies use performance appraisal for more than one purpose.[5] This reflects the widespread recognition that performance appraisal, if done effectively, can increase productivity, develop bench strength for future growth, and decrease organizational costs.

It's essential that the team agree on the purposes of performance review before embarking on the design of an appraisal instrument. It's also essential to recognize and take action to address conflicting purposes served by the same process. If pay is tied to performance, for example, the team will have to take precautions to ensure that discussions are open and candid so the developmental purpose can be adequately served.

At the very least, the tool should serve a performance management and developmental function that lets people know what's expected at the beginning of the appraisal period and how performance will be appraised. Then, periodically throughout the appraisal period, feedback is given on how well the expectations are being met and what to do to improve performance. At the end of the performance management cycle, overall performance can be appraised and used to support decisions in development planning.

We'll discuss these issues in more depth; but first, let's examine four common patterns of team performance appraisals.

Behavior Model of Team Appraisal Patterns

The Model of Team Appraisal Patterns consists of two factors:
1. Clear and specific direction and feedback
2. Participation in appraising performance

Clear and Specific Direction and Feedback
An effective appraisal process provides clear and specific direction and feedback. Direction is clear if people know exactly what's expected and how performance is to be evaluated. Feedback is clear if it provides specific information about what to do more of, less of, or differently going forward.

Participation in Appraising Performance
Effective performance appraisal involves active participation, self-assessment, and self-discovery of strengths and improvement areas. As a result, there's commitment to maintaining or building on strengths and addressing improvement areas.

The Model of Team Appraisal Patterns (Exhibit 14-1) shows how both dimensions — clear and specific direction and feedback and participation in appraising performance — combine to form four appraisal patterns.

Following are examples of how team members describe each pattern:
- *Forming*: We don't conduct appraisals. We just go along assuming what we are doing is acceptable and not worrying much about how we'll operate in the future.
- *Storming*: Our appraisals are specific and usually given by the team leader or a dominant member when things get out of hand. They come across as harsh, blaming, fault finding, and biting.
- *Norming*: We are actively involved in participating in our appraisals but the feedback is typically general and positive. Rarely do we discuss negative performance and address improvement plans.
- *Performing*: Our appraisals are candid, constructive, and balanced with negative and positive feedback. We are encouraged to participate actively and critique our own performance so the outcome is generally accepted and we act on plans for building on strengths and addressing areas for improvement.

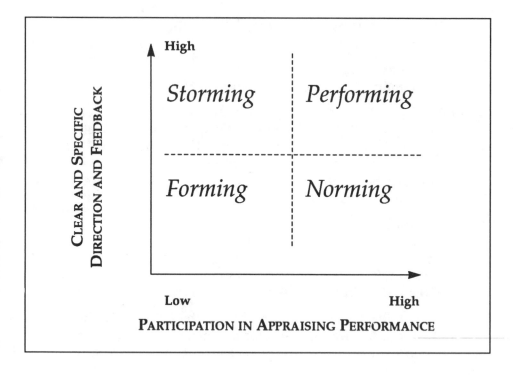

Exhibit 14-1: Team Appraisal Patterns

The Performance Management Cycle

To be effective, performance appraisal must be more than a once-a-year event. It must be ongoing — a cyclical process of:

- *Clarifying Expectations* — so people know what is expected and how performance will be appraised.
- *Conducting Periodic Reviews* — so people know how they're performing and what they can do to improve performance.
- *Conducting Overall Review* — documents performance throughout the appraisal period to support decisions about compensation and personal development planning.

Exhibit 14-2 illustrates the performance management cycle.

Clarifying Expectations

At the beginning of the appraisal period, the team establishes expectations for the team and each member. These expectations typically cover a period spanning anywhere from 3 to 12 months and specify *what's* to be accomplished (goals) and *how* the team members will go about their work (behavior standards or competencies). Finally, the team sets interim milestones and follow-up dates to review performance.

Conducting Periodic Reviews
Throughout the appraisal period, touch-base meetings are held to review progress and completed assignments. Each team member receives feedback on behavior strengths and improvement areas. Positive feedback is given to maintain performance and motivate it to higher levels. Corrective action is taken to get performance (goals and behavior) back on track.

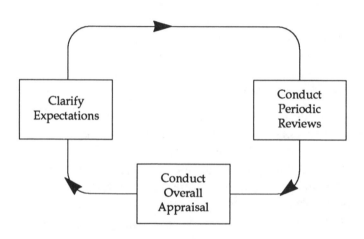

xhibit 14-2: Performance Management Cycle

Conducting the Overall Review
If the team does a good job of reviewing and managing performance throughout the appraisal period, the overall review is simply a documentation of what was discussed all along. The team reviews and documents its collective accomplishments as well as the behavior and contribution of each member. Then the cycle starts again.

Benefits of a Performance Management Cycle
A performance management cycle can eliminate many of the problems inherent in once-a-year appraisals. First, going into the cycle people know exactly what's expected. The ground rules and expectations are clearly laid out. In essence, a contract is established between the team and each member.

Second, feedback is usually more candid and specific since the touch-base sessions are used as progress checks and the basis for making performance improvement rather than as final judgments upon which personnel decisions are made.

Third, it's in the best interest of the team to support each member with accurate feedback, coaching, and encouragement. This is so each individual has every opportunity to improve performance and contribution to the team before the overall review.

Finally, the frequent feedback is educational and motivational. It's educational in that it informs people what to do less of or differently. It's motivational in that positive behaviors are recognized, which increases the probability that they are continued or performed more often.

Appraising the *What* and the *How*

The question which inevitably arises in performance appraisal is what do we appraise. The answer is both the *what* and the *how*. The *what* refers to the goals, objectives, and quantitative key results that the team and each individual is expected to contribute. The *how* refers to the performance behaviors that are important in promoting teamwork and achieving the team goals in a collaborative fashion.

Supposing that at the first progress review meeting two team members are falling short of their goals to provide high quality and on-time delivery of finished drilled sheets to their internal customers. One team member is a bit reserved and hesitant to work with the internal customers. Another is abrasive and turns off the internal customers. Since maintaining close working relationships with internal customers is essential to meeting the goals, reviewing the behavior standards helps pinpoint the cause of the problem so corrective action can be taken. The *how* (behavior) helps diagnose why the *what* (goals) are not being achieved.

Here's another example. Terry is quite aggressive. He is notorious as a "mover and shaker." After joining the team, he quickly took the bull by the horns and exceeded all his job goals. But, in doing so, he disrupted the work of others and caused several teammates to fall short of their goals. He was excellent at getting results but dismal as a team player. By appraising the *what* and the *how*, Terry got a dose of self-awareness and an understanding that total performance is not simply *what* you produce but includes style of performance and teamwork.

These two scenarios illustrate an important point:

Total Performance = *What's* accomplished + *How* the team member goes about accomplishing goals and expectations.

The *what* relates to goals and job results each team member must achieve if the team as a whole is to succeed. The *how* relates to the important behaviors that, if performed effectively, will lead to the desired goals and stronger teamwork. Together, the *what* and the *how* define total performance.

This is why a team performance appraisal should address both the *what* and the *how*. The goals and behaviors can be appraised in the same tool on the same schedule within the performance management cycle or in separate tools on separate schedules. But it is essential that total performance be appraised.

Clarifying Goals and Expectations

In the chapter on goal setting, we discussed SMART goals and how to establish them. It is imperative that, at the beginning of the appraisal period, team goals are established and translated into individual accountabilities with time lines. This is so each team member knows what's expected and how he or she will contribute to the team. One way to do this is to first develop team goals. Then, for each team goal establish an action plan. The action plan specifies who's to do what by when to help the team achieve its goals.

It's essential that each item on the action plan be assigned to only one person. With multiple accountabilities for the same action item, several people are responsible but no one is accountable. If it is difficult to establish a single accountability for an action item, that means it is too broad. Break it down into subactions that can be assigned to individuals. This helps clarify who's to do what and how the team members are to work together to achieve the team goals.

It's also essential that each member's goals be measurable. If they are not, expect confusion when it comes to appraising performance. Often the team is better off not including poorly defined or difficult to measure goals.

Clarifying Behavioral Expectations

In addition to establishing individual accountabilities for action items and results, it is important to clarify behavioral expectations. Behavioral expectations define *how* the team members are to go about working together and relate to things like communicating openly, participating in problem solving and decision making, providing timely support and resources, and the like.

Behavioral expectations are observable behaviors or competencies that clearly define what it means to be a strong team player. They are especially useful for giving feedback to the team members and continuously developing performance and potential. You'll never develop into a high-performance team without clear behavioral expectations that are periodically reviewed as part of the team appraisal process.

Behavioral expectations must be specific — that is, an easily observed single aspect of performance behavior. "Works well with statistical and narrative reports" is neither specific (it doesn't define what "well" means) and is not a single aspect of performance (a person might be effective with narrative but poor with statistical reports). Keep behavioral expectations specific and one dimensional.

Sample Behavioral Expectations

Here is a collection of specific behavioral expectations that a team can adapt to define standards for performance. The team members should individually review the list and decide on the most important behavior categories and performance behaviors. Then, as a team, reach consensus on a profile of team member excellence. The profile of anywhere from three to five categories and three to five behaviors within each is used as a template to review and give feedback on how each team member is performing.

Gets Things Done

- Acts quickly to move ideas and plans to action.
- Keeps focused on the task and the desired results of projects.
- Perseveres through roadblocks and barriers to get things done.
- "Rolls up sleeves" and helps team accomplish its objectives.
- Works persistently with attentiveness to detail.

Promotes Open Communication

- Encourages others to express their opinions and ideas.
- Listens to fully understand the ideas and views of others.
- Presents pertinent ideas and information clearly and concisely.
- Promotes discussion by probing and building on the ideas of others.
- Says what he/she really thinks and feels.

Displays Dependability and Reliability

- Fulfills commitments and obligations to others.
- Follows through on tasks in a timely manner.
- Can be depended upon to meet schedules and deadlines.
- Pitches in to complete what needs to be done to meet project deadlines.
- Accepts personal responsibility and ownership for completing projects.

Supports Others

- Keeps people informed on topics related to the team task.
- Provides advice and assistance to help others do their job.
- Gives constructive feedback about how to improve performance.
- Shares resources freely with others.
- Promotes a "one for all and all for one" climate of sharing and openness.

Displays Adaptability and Flexibility

- Demonstrates flexibility when project priorities change.
- Displays flexibility in meeting the changing needs of clients.
- Adapts quickly to diverse projects and people.
- Willingly accepts new tasks.
- Quickly learns and applies new skills and techniques.

Maintains a Strong Service Orientation

- Promotes good relationships with customers.
- Is responsive to the needs of customers.
- Handles inquiries and complaints in a professional manner.
- Strives to under promise and over deliver to customers.
- Solicits feedback from customers to continually improve service.

Is Productive and Quality Conscious

- Adds value to the team's products and services.
- Participates actively in team meetings.
- Contributes creative ideas to the team.
- Maintains high standards for quality.
- Does things right the first time.

Contributes to Team Problem Solving and Decision Making

- Helps clarify the problem and explore problem causes.
- Contributes well-thought-out ideas to solve problems and make decisions.
- Considers the immediate and long-term impact of alternatives.
- Pushes for the most rational and sound decisions and solutions.
- Helps develop practical action plans for implementing decisions.

Is a Team Player
• Puts the goals of the team ahead of personal agendas.
• Is open-minded to new ideas and approaches.
• Willingly accepts and acts on constructive criticism from others.
• Seeks advice/assistance to improve work method and job results.
• Cooperates fully and seeks ways to help team members.

Establishing an Appraisal Tool

Once the team selects the behavior standards, it then develops an appraisal tool. Most appraisal instruments contain three sections: (a) team member goals, (b) behavioral expectations, and (c) overall evaluation.

There are two kinds of team member goals — business and behavioral. Business goals are established from team goals and relate to what each member is to achieve if the team is to succeed. Behavioral goals relate to the specific skill improvement or performance development goals the members must achieve if they are to grow and contribute more fully to the team. An example of a behavioral goal is, "Develops facilitation skills to the extent that 9 of 10 meetings end on time and meeting evaluation scores show that participants are, on average, *very satisfied* to *extremely satisfied* on all factors."

The team rates each member's goal attainment using a scale that ranges from *Exceeds goal level*, to *Meets goal level*, to *Below goal level*.

Behavioral expectations are rated using a frequency scale such as *Almost Always, Very Often, Frequently, Sometimes*, and *Rarely*. Or, a Likert scale can be used, such as *Strongly Agree, Agree, Agree More than Disagree, Disagree*, and *Disagree Strongly*.

Finally, overall performance is evaluated by considering both what was accomplished and the extent that the behavioral expectations were displayed. The team should agree on how to weight the two sections to arrive at an overall performance rating.

Generally, a 70/30 or 60/40 percent weight ratio is assigned to goals versus behavioral expectations. This should be discussed and agreed to at the beginning of the appraisal cycle so people know what's expected and how their performance will be evaluated.

On the following pages (Exhibit 14-3) is an example of a performance appraisal tool. The team should develop a tool that meets their needs. It may be like the one shown with goals and behavioral expectations included in the same form. Or they may be separated. The best thing to do is adopt a "Do it, Fix it, Try it" attitude. Develop a tool, then try it out. Keep what works and change what doesn't. You'll continually improve the tool and make it practical and useful for the purposes it is designed to serve.

Exhibit 14-3: Sample Team Appraisal

Name:	Appraisal Period	
	From:	To:

Title:	Department:

Part 1: Business and Behavioral Goals

- List business and behavioral goals below for the appraisal period specified above.
- Ensure goals are measurable — include measurement methods of quantity, quality, cost, time lines.
- Touch base to assess progress noting: "O" = Off Target-Corrective Action Taken or "T" = On Target-No Action Necessary.
- Review overall goal attainment using ratings of: *Below goal level, Meets goal level, Exceeds goal level.*
- Include comments or explanation for touch base or overall review in the space provided.

Business Goals	Touch Base	Overall Review

Business Goals Comments/Explanation:

Behavioral Goals	Touch Base	Overall Review

Behavioral Goals Comments/Explanation:

Part 2: Behavioral Expectations

- Review behavioral expectations at the beginning of the appraisal period to ensure clarity.
- Touch base to assess behavioral strengths and improvement areas — Note at least three Strengths (S) and at least three Improvement areas (I).
- Evaluate overall Behavioral Expectations by circling: "AA" = Almost Always, "VO" = Very Often, "U" = Usually, "S" = Sometimes, "AN" = Almost Never.
- Include comments or explanation in space provided.

Behavioral Expectations

Is a Team Player	Touch Base	Overall Rating
• Puts the goals of the team ahead of personal agendas.		AN S U VO AA
• Is open-minded to new ideas and approaches.		AN S U VO AA
• Willingly accepts and acts on constructive criticism from others.		AN S U VO AA
• Seeks advice/assistance to improve work method and job results.		AN S U VO AA
• Cooperates fully and seeks ways to help team members.		AN S U VO AA

Comments/Explantion:

Contributes to Team Problem Solving	Touch Base	Overall Rating
• Helps clarify the problem and explore problem causes.		AN S U VO AA
• Offers well-thought-out ideas to solve problems/make decisions.		AN S U VO AA
• Considers the immediate and long-term impact of alternatives.		AN S U VO AA
• Pushes for the most rational and sound decisions and solutions.		AN S U VO AA
• Helps develop practical action plans for implementing decisions.		AN S U VO AA

Comments/Explantion:

Is Productive and Quality Conscious	Touch Base	Overall Rating
• Adds value to the team's products and services.		AN S U VO AA
• Participates actively in team meetings.		AN S U VO AA
• Contributes creative ideas to the team.		AN S U VO AA
• Maintains high standards for quality.		AN S U VO AA
• Does things right the first time.		AN S U VO AA

Comments/Explantion:

Part 3: Overall Evaluation
- Consider appraisal of goals and behavioral expectations to derive an overall evaluation.
- Use categories of: *Exceeds Requirements, Meets Requirements, Below Requirements.*
- List Major Strengths and Improvement Areas.
- Include comments or explanation in space provided.
- Translate Improvement Areas into Behavioral Goals for the next Appraisal Period.

Overall Evaluation
❏ Below Requirements   ❏ Meets Requirements   ❏ Exceeds Requirements
Comments/Explanation:
Strengths:
Improvement Areas:
Individual(s) Participating in Appraisal:
Received By: _____   Date: _____ Approved By: _____   Date: _____

Who Should Appraise Performance?

There are several alternatives to the question: Who should appraise performance? Here are six options:

1. the supervisor
2. self
3. team members
4. internal and/or external customers
5. direct reports
6. some combination of the above[6]

To appraise behavioral expectations, probably the best source of information is from peers. It's not surprising that this is the most accurate source of information.[7] Peers interact most closely with one another and are in the best position to observe and report behavior.

In most situations, self-ratings should be encouraged to ensure participation in the process, open discussion of where perceptions agree and disagree, and commitment to development plans.[8]

Customers — recipients of the team's work products and services — are often in the best position to appraise goals and objectives. Supervisors also may have good insight into the quality of the team's performance against goals.

At the beginning of the appraisal period, examine each goal and ask the question: Who's in the best position to provide an objective evaluation and thorough feedback about this goal? Then, enlist their help in reviewing performance and providing feedback to the team. Ask them to give you interim reviews according to the schedule of the performance management cycle to ensure you have every opportunity to achieve your goals and enhance performance.

Team Participation in the Appraisal Process

Active participation in each phase of the performance management cycle is essential for an effective appraisal process — one that is accurate, thorough, and involving.

Setting Expectations

Conduct a goal-setting meeting as described in Chapter 6. Each team member should individually consider what he or she believes the team goals should be. Through a consensus process reach agreement on team goals. Then, translate team goals into individual accountabilities using an action planning process.

Conducting Periodic Reviews

Through periodic reviews the team reviews its progress on goals and each team member receives specific feedback on behavioral strengths and improvement areas.

Each team member should prepare for the meeting in advance by: (a) reviewing progress on his or her own goals, and (b) considering the performance of all other team members to identify two or three strengths and two or three improvement areas.

The meeting begins with each person reporting on progress toward their goals — is it "on target" or "off target?" The team may ask questions for clarification or comment on the reports. If necessary the team will help problem solve actions to take to get goals back on track. Each team member records the progress review information on the appraisal form.

After progress on all individual goals has been reported, the team should have a good view of how it is doing and what it needs to do more of, less of, or differently going forward. Now, the focus shifts to behavioral expectations.

Each team member should prepare a flip chart listing the behavioral expectations. All other team members, in a round-robin fashion, report the two or three strengths of the team member being appraised and why they are strengths. Then, the team members give feedback on improvement areas and why they feel these areas are in need of improvement. The team member receiving the feedback does not speak through this process — he or she simply records the feedback on the flip chart indicating with check marks where the team members reported strengths and improvement areas.

Once the feedback from all team members is on the flip chart, the team discusses and reaches agreement on the major strengths and improvement areas — no more than two or three of each. At that point, the recipient of the appraisal can ask questions for clarification. It is not productive to disagree or try to argue with the other team members. They are simply reporting their perceptions of the team member's behavior.

Finally, the team recommends action steps for building on strengths and addressing improvement areas. The recipient takes careful notes and can make comments to the team about the value of the feedback and the usefulness of the recommendations. The recipient records the feedback on behavioral strengths and improvement areas on the appraisal form in the column labeled "touch base."

Conducting the Overall Review

At the overall review, the process is much the same as with the touch-base review. Each team member reports on goal attainment and the team responds. Then each team member receives feedback on behavioral strengths and improvement areas. If the team has done a good job with touch-base sessions, this overall review should be little more than a formality — a recap of what was discussed all along.

Giving Feedback

Feedback should be specific, balanced, constructive, and candid.

Specific feedback means it focuses on concrete and observable behavior, not inferences about traits or personality characteristics.

Balanced feedback means there is both positive and negative feedback. Positive feedback should be specific and inform the team member exactly what to continue doing or do more of. Negative feedback should be educational — letting the team member know what to do less or differently and why. Feedback that is one-sided — all positive or negative — does not reflect an accurate view of the team member's performance.

Constructive feedback is delivered in a way that is helpful and enabling, focusing on behavior and future ways to improve performance. Destructive feedback focuses on the person and comes across as harsh, fault finding, and oriented to the past.

Candid feedback is saying what you really think and see. It's telling it like it is. Feedback that is not candid is saying what people want to hear or what's politically acceptable. Feedback that is not candid is either general and vague or does very little to clarify what the team member should do to change and improve performance.

Make every effort to provide specific, balanced, constructive, and candid feedback. And provide feedback in a timely fashion. Specific, balanced, constructive, candid, and timely feedback is a tremendous motivational and developmental tool. Without good feedback, motivation diminishes and the tremendous developmental value is lost.

Promoting Candor

Teamwide candor is important for ensuring open discussion and sharing of perceptions about performance. Because of the importance of providing feedback candidly, it's vital that candor and confidentiality be discussed prior to appraisal and feedback meetings.

Think about the upcoming feedback meeting and how you and your team will be:
- *Candid* — saying what you really think and feel, telling it like it is. Candor should be helpful and constructive, not vague, general, or destructive.
- *Confidential* — keeping the information in the room, protected and respected, restricted for exclusive use of the team.

Each team member should individually complete a candor rating using the worksheet on the following page. Check one box for each question. "None" means there are no concerns about candor or confidentiality. "Some" means there are.

After everyone has completed the ratings, post them on the flip chart. Discuss the ratings and get all the issues out on the table. Develop procedures or ground rules for addressing them before the appraisal meeting.

Discuss the value of the appraisal meeting and why it is important to have candor, confidentiality, and good feedback. Then monitor the appraisal process closely to ensure candor remains high. A candor monitor can be assigned the role of periodically critiquing the candor level and reporting specific observations to the team.

Team Candor and Confidentiality Worksheet

1. **My Candor.** Do you foresee any issues
    getting in the way of being candid when   ❏ None   ❏ Some
    you are giving or receiving feedback?

    Comments:

2. **Their Candor.** Do you foresee any issues
    getting in the way of being candid when   ❏ None   ❏ Some
    others are giving or receiving feedback?

    Comments:

3. **Confidentiality.** Do you foresee any issues
    concerning confidentiality relative to the   ❏ None   ❏ Some
    appraisal process?

    Comments:

**Actions, ground rules, or procedures we need to promote
strong candor and confidentiality:**

Endnotes

1. D. L. DeVries, A. M. Morrison, S. L. Shullman, M. L. Gerlach. *Performance Appraisal on the Line.* New York: John Wiley & Sons, 1981.

2. A. H. Locher & K. S. Teel. Assessment: Appraisal Trends. *Personnel Journal,* September 1988, 139-144.

3. G. P. Latham & K. N. Wexley. *Increasing Productivity Through Performance Appraisal.* Reading: Addison-Wesley, 1980.

4. J. N. Cleveland, K. R. Murphy & R. E. Williams. Multiple Uses of Performance Appraisal: Prevalence and Correlates. *Journal of Applied Psychology,* 1989, 130-135.

5. A. H. Locher & K. S. Teel. Assessment: Appraisal Trends. *Personnel Journal,* September 1988, 139-144.

6. G. P. Latham & K. N. Wexley. *Increasing Productivity Through Performance Appraisal.* Reading: Addison-Wesley, 1980.

7. G. M. McEvoy & P. Buller. User Acceptance of Peer Appraisals in an Industrial Setting. *Personnel Psychology,* 1987, 785-797.

8. H. H. Meyer. A Solution to the Performance Appraisal Enigma. *Academy of Management Executive,* 1991, 68-75.

Chapter

15

Improving Work Process and Work Flow

*"Forget the pyramid. Smash the hierarchy, break the
company into its key processes, and create teams from
different departments to manage them."*

> —John Byrne, Senior Writer
> Business Week[1]

"It seems like the dust just settled from the last reorganization and now I'm hearing rumors of another," Kim announced nervously. "This one's different," Jack said with some sarcasm. "This one is called delayering."

No matter where you work, it's likely your company has been "downsized," "rightsized," "delayered," or, to use today's vernacular, "reengineered." The idea is simple and quite appealing. Since work flows horizontally through the organization and across functions, why have functions at all? A functional organization with silo-like structures causes work to unnaturally flow up and down through the hierarchy as it is passed sequentially from function to function.

This chapter is about analyzing work flow to improve efficiency and business results. We'll address the methods for looking at work in disciplined ways and the stunningly vast opportunities that can be found to eliminate unnecessary and non-value-adding work.

Why not dismantle the hierarchy and organize around core business processes? Why not empower the people who do the work with authority to make decisions about the work? Do supervisory structures really add value?

These are the questions being posed with increasing frequency in the chambers of many chief executives. And many organizations are learning they can gain speed, shed unnecessary work, and deliver higher-quality products and services if they adopt a new organization model — the horizontal corporation.

It's a simple matter of breaking down functional barriers and restructuring around three to five core processes of the business. Find and eliminate work that fails to add value and competitive advantage. Use teams as the building blocks of the organization, empowered to perform entire work processes and held accountable for measurable goals like quality, efficiency, and service.

General Electric's John Welch, Jr., speaks of the "boundaryless" organization that has helped reduce costs, shorten cycle times, and increase responsiveness to customers.[2] At DuPont, the focus is on creating a seamless system — tearing down the functional and departmental boundaries that increase the frequency of "disconnects" and problems in "handoffs."[3]

AlliedSignal's Lawrence Bossidy argues that almost any process is susceptible to improvement and for those that have been around for a while the improvement opportunities are huge. "We can't have fewer initiatives," he says, "but we can sure be open-minded about eliminating what doesn't add value." Just look at the results. AlliedSignal was bleeding when Bossidy arrived. It has since boosted earnings per share by 74 percent and stock price by 145 percent.[4]

This chapter focuses on how to rethink outmoded structures — how to take an open-minded, systematic, and disciplined look at the way things get done.

Road Map

Rationale for Changes in Structure and Workflow

What is wrong with the picture shown in Exhibit 15-1?

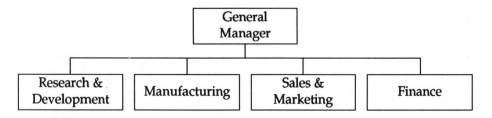

Exhibit 15-1: Traditional Functional Structure

Consultants Geary Rummler and Alan Brache are quick to point out three missing elements — what's done, for whom, and how. First, it doesn't show the customers. Second, it doesn't show the products and services provided. And finally, there is no sense of how the work flows — how the organization develops, produces, and delivers the product or service to the customers.[5]

This may be acceptable for a small organization. But for a large and complex organization, this view of things does not help continuously improve product quality, operational efficiency, and customer service. Now examine Exhibit 15-2 — the horizontal view of the organization.

The systems or horizontal view shown in Exhibit 15-2 includes the missing ingredients — customers, products, and work flow — enabling us to see how things actually get done. It shows the horizontal processes that cut across functional lines.

Exhibit 15-3 shows another perspective on the workflow.

This functional form of organization (Exhibit 15-3) is based on the "expert" model. Each function is composed of functional experts who do their thing up and down the silo-like structure and then throw their work over the wall to another function. Finance prepares its detailed statements and throws them over the wall to other functions who must make sense of them. Engineering prepares elaborate designs and throws them over the wall to manufacturing, who has to make them work. Purchasing buys as cheaply as possible and throws supplies over the wall to manufacturing, who must make do with low-cost but not necessarily high-quality materials.

Research on Market Trends and Competitive Activity

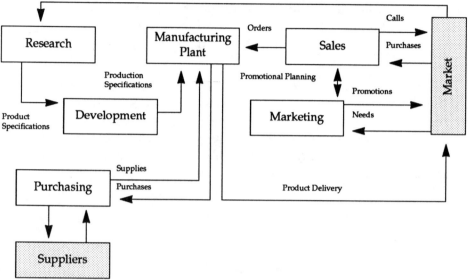

Exhibit 15-2: Overview of Horizontal Processes

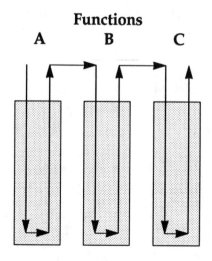

Exhibit 15-3: Work Flow in a Functional Structure

The entire work process is inefficient — the vertical flow of work and the numerous handoffs slow down cycle times, which increases costs. The creativity, initiative, ownership, and accountability is minimal. And the possibility for quality problems and rework is increased.

The silo structure, while optimizing functionalization, suboptimizes the organization as a whole. It forces managers to resolve lower-level issues, taking their time away from higher-priority strategic concerns and managing teamwork. Lower-level employees, who could be resolving these issues, take less responsibility for them than they might since they see themselves as mere implementers and information providers.[6]

Exhibit 15-4 shows the natural flow of work.

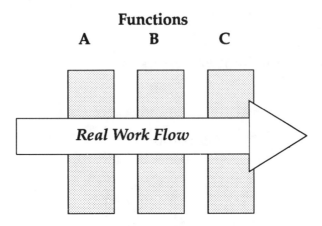

Exhibit 15-4: Real Work Flow

As is seen in Exhibit 15-4, the unnatural and unnecessary boundaries between the internal and external customers and suppliers are reduced or eliminated. The functional experts are replaced by process teams who have the wherewithal to continuously improve product quality, operational efficiency, and customer service.

This value-adding, customer-focused organization is created in two ways — by totally reorganizing around processes, or by creating secondary organizations that are horizontal and cross-functional like product development teams. In the next sections we'll address how.

Business Processes Defined

One term that gives corporate managers a lot of difficulty is "business process." In this section, we'll define the term thoroughly and operationally.

According to Michael Hammer and James Champy, business reengineering gurus, a business process is "...a collection of activities that takes one or more kinds of input and creates an output that is of value to the customer."[7] An example is developing a new product. By combining the tasks that form the whole process and empowering a team to perform them, you reduce or eliminate the problems associated with functional handoffs and disconnects and increase overall efficiency and quality.

Geary Rummler and Alan Brache view a process as a "value chain." A process is a "...series of steps designed to produce a product or service. Most processes are cross-functional and viewing them as value chains means that, in the development or delivery of a product or service, each step in the process should add value, in customers' terms, to the previous step.[8]

Naming Processes

Business processes are natural business activities that are invisible and unnamed because they are often fragmented and obscured by the functional structure. Processes tend to be unmanaged — managers are accountable for functional or departmental affairs, but no one is responsible for the whole job.

One way to define and name a business process is to name the beginning and end states. For example, instead of using the functional name "Production," call the process *procurement to shipment*. Instead of referring to the "Product Development" department, call it *idea to prototype*. Rather than refer to the "Service Department," refer to the process *inquiry to resolution*.[9]

Here's how we named five priority business processes at a large manufacturer by labeling their beginning and ending states:
- Strategy development: market needs/requirement to business strategy
- Product development: concept to finished product
- Sales: prospect to buyer
- Sales administration: order to payment
- Distribution: order to delivery

Two Factors Defining a Process Improvement Initiative
Further delineation of the term process is provided by McKinsey consultants Gene Hall, Jim Rosenthal, and Judy Wade.[10] They focus on two factors — process *breadth* and process *depth* — that are crucial to consider in any process improvement initiative.

Process *breadth* refers to the scope of activities used to define a process. In the narrowest definition, a single activity in a single function such as accounts payable is the focus of attention. More broadly defined, a process might include operations composed of numerous activities spanning across many functions, like product development or order fulfillment.

Process *breadth* is important because the more activities included in the process, the more likely the improvements will have a significant and lasting impact on the business. More opportunities exist to reduce delays, decrease errors, and enhance efficiency in more broadly defined processes. The challenge is to find the two to three core processes that contribute fully to adding value for the customer and define the company's competitive advantage. Then begin addressing those processes that are most severely falling short of meeting customer expectations, achieving management objectives, and providing a differential competitive advantage.

The second factor is *depth*, which refers to the degree of change in at least six crucial organizational systems: (1) structure, (2) roles and responsibilities of the key players, (3) performance measures, appraisal procedures, and reward systems, (4) management information systems, (5) shared values, and (6) skills.

A successful process improvement initiative must redesign the structure to reduce redundancies, handoffs, and non-value-added activities. Then it must provide clear direction for the team in terms of expectations, appraisal measures and methods, and rewards. Information systems must be realigned to provide timely feedback on progress and results. Values about quality and customer service must be instilled by top management. And finally, the team members must be equipped with the skills to work together and continuously improve operational efficiency.

Without adequate *breadth* and *depth*, a process improvement initiative will fail to deliver the business results that motivated the change in the first place.

Redesigning Work

Work redesign is aimed at fixing an ailing process, redesigning an existing process to make it even better, or designing an entirely new process. The steps in process improvement are:

1. Identify Critical Result Areas

Typically senior management identifies opportunities to improve existing products or to develop new products or services, enhance responsiveness to customers and markets or create new markets, and establish or increase the company's differential competitive advantage. A critical result is what the company must do exceptionally well if it is to efficiently develop and deliver high-quality products and services in a way that maximizes customer satisfaction and differentiates the company from the competition.

Examples of critical result areas might be to reduce time from idea to prototype from six months to four, cut production costs by 10 percent, and achieve the capability to provide same-day delivery of a "hot item" to the customer. These Critical Result Areas usually relate to a problem or opportunity impinging on the strategic direction of the company.

2. Define Important Process(es)

Define the process(es) that have the greatest potential for helping the company achieve the critical result areas. An example of a process is all the activities within product development, marketing, creative, manufacturing, packaging, and distribution of Product X — all the functions that must coordinate to improve product development and delivery of Product X.

By defining important processes, senior management is seeking to:
- Reduce the number of interfaces and handoffs to a minimum so goals for quality and efficiency are achieved.
- Produce the closest proximity of internal customers and suppliers.
- Establish clarity of roles, responsibilities, authorities, and coordination requirements.

3. Select the Process Team

Select individuals from the various functions who have working knowledge of a key process task or activity. Ensure each key task in the process has an individual who fully understands it and possesses the competency and commitment to work on the team. In addition, you should identify a facilitator or "process owner" — someone to guide and facilitate the efforts of the team. If you end up with more than 10 to 12 team members, the process may be too broadly defined, in which case you'll cycle back to Step 2.

4. Provide Team Training

Begin with setting direction for the team (mission, goals, roles, and responsibilities), then provide skills training in team functions like meetings, decision making, problem solving, and conflict management.

5. Develop a Process Map of the *Current* Situation

A process map is developed by having the facilitator or process owner interview the team members and drawing a "straw man" map. Then it is presented to the team for review and refinement.

6. Analyze Disconnects and Handoff Problems

As the team refines the *current* situation process map, it should list the disconnects, delays, redundancies, non-value-adding steps, and delays that may affect the critical result areas. Use a problem-solving process (see Chapter 10) to determine why they are occurring and how to address them.

7. Develop a Process Map of the *Ideal* Situation

By streamlining the chain of events and ensuring each activity adds value, an *ideal* situation process map is defined. Then it is compared to the critical result areas to ensure that the results will be achieved if the new process configuration succeeds.

8. Establish Measurement Methods for Each Critical Result Area and Each Subprocess

Here are some examples of subprocesses and measurement methods for an order fulfillment process.

• Order Received	100% complete and accurate
• Order Entered	Same day received
• Credit Checked	Within 24 hours
• Production Scheduled	Two errors per 1,000
• Packages Checked	Two reworks per 10,000
• Order Shipped	Within 3 days of receipt

Most measurements can be defined in terms of quality, quantity, cost, and time.

9. Present Plans and Recommendations to Steering Committee for Approval

Oftentimes a "Steering Committee" is assembled early in the effort to provide general direction to the process teams, monitor their performance, and ensure that roadblocks and barriers that can get in the way of achieving the critical result areas are minimized. This committee is usually composed of members of senior management and function heads. Here the Steering Committee must sign off on the plans and recommendations made by the process team and commit to fully supporting their efforts.

Analyzing Relationships, Process States, and Work Flow

Structural changes and business process improvement initiatives must begin with an analysis of the *current* situation. There are three analytical methods for doing this — relationship analysis, process states analysis, and work flow analysis — and most teams use all three.

Relationship mapping occurs at the macro level within the organization and involves charting the input-output relationships among functions and departments within functions. Process states show the major changes in states as inputs are transformed into outputs. At the micro level, mapping the work flow shows the specific tasks and activities that departments perform to achieve state changes and to convert inputs to outputs for a specific process.

Relationship Mapping

A relationship map is used to show the work flow among departments so we can:

- Understand how work gets done in the functional and departmental scheme of things — determine if all functions are in place and the appropriate flow of inputs and outputs is occurring between functions.
- Identify missing, unnecessary, delayed, or misdirected connections between inputs and outputs.
- Eliminate disconnects and handoff malfunctions.
- Determine alternatives to structuring the organizational wiring.

In constructing a *current* situation relationship map, for example, we might determine that production forecasts are being done by finance without input from sales and manufacturing. Or, we may find that marketing does not participate in forecasting sales, and multiple functions are responsible for various aspects of customer service but none is fully accountable.

To develop a Relationship Map, you draw and label arrows that illustrate the internal customer-supplier relationships — the input and output flow — among all line and staff functions. The example in Exhibit 15-5 was shown earlier as an example of a Relationship Map.

Process State (Transformational) Mapping

As input moves through the work system, it becomes transformed — value is added which changes the physical state into an output. Here's an illustration:

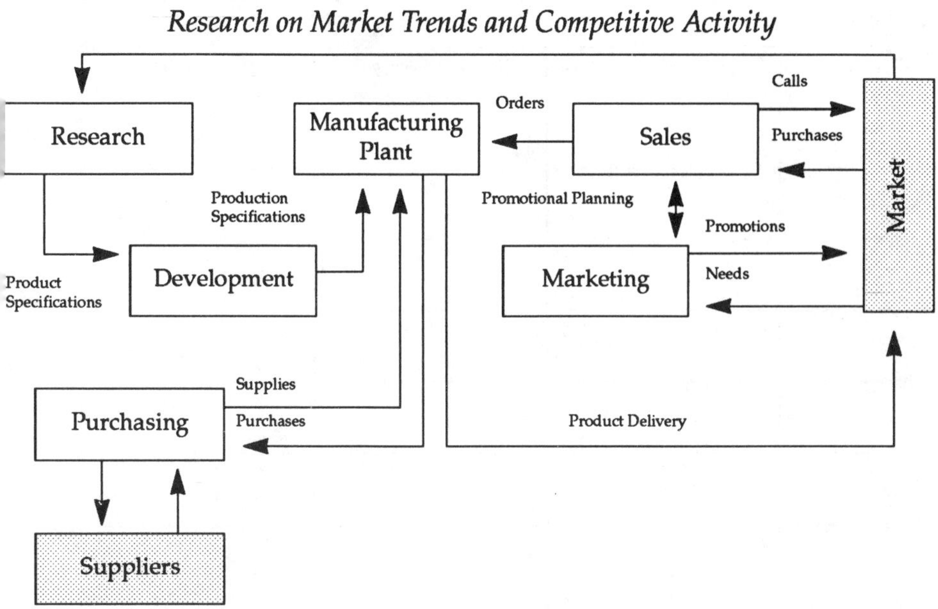

Research on Market Trends and Competitive Activity

Exhibit 15-5: Relationship Map

Input   **Sales Forecasts by Territory Manager**

State Changes
1. Receive data by fax from field offices
2. Input data into computer
3. Compute consolidated sales by product and region
4. Compute cost of sales, cost of goods sold, and profit
5. Break out projections by month
6. Print report

Output   **Sales Forecast and Budgets**

The purpose of State Change Mapping is to identify problems in the transformation process — delays, unneeded activities, redundancies — in the process of transforming inputs to outputs.

A worksheet like that shown in Exhibit 15-6 is often useful for analyzing the various transformational processes between all inputs and outputs in a business process.

Work Process:			
State Change	**Required Actions**	**Other Actions**	**By Whom**

Exhibit 15-6: State Change (Transformation) Worksheet

Completing this worksheet allows you to search each State Change for opportunities or problems in the activities or actions involved in the transformational process. Opportunities or problems may be immediately visible — opportunities to streamline or shortcut the current process. There also may be problems apparent in the column labeled "Other Actions." Here there may be unneeded actions or unnecessary delays that need fixing. Finally, opportunities or problems may surface in the "By Whom" column, where no accountability or multiple accountabilities are apparent.

Process Work Flow Mapping

Process Work Flow Mapping is the most detailed view of how the work flows through the organization. It provides a visual picture of how the process works — the activities, steps, and inter-relationships that go into a process.

The first step is to agree on the symbols that will be used to map the process. The common ones are illustrated in Exhibit 15-7.

Meaning	Symbol
Decision	Diamond 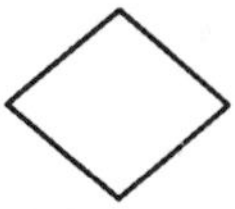
Work Action or Activity	Rectangle 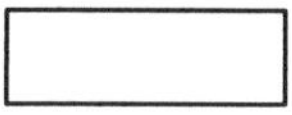
Transporting or Moving	Arrow 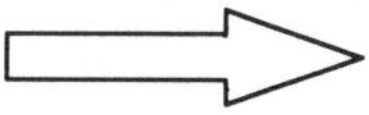
Delay	Circle 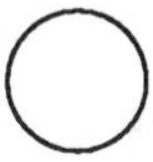
Inspect or Review	Triangle 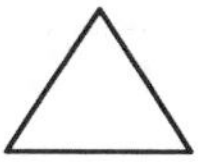

Exhibit 15-7: Common Flowchart Symbols

You can make up additional symbols for specific types of activities if desired. Just make sure all team members understand what the symbols signify.

Next, ask the team members to use the symbols to chart the activities, decisions, and steps that occur to produce the state changes and transformation of inputs to outputs. Some teams write the activities on 3-by-5 note cards and tape them to a wall. This provides a visual image of the flow of work and allows the team to easily make changes when constructing an *ideal* process map.

An example of a flowchart of an order fulfillment process is shown in Exhibit 15-8.

By charting relationships, work flow, and state changes, you'll see problems and opportunities that, if addressed, can significantly enhance productivity, quality, and efficiency.

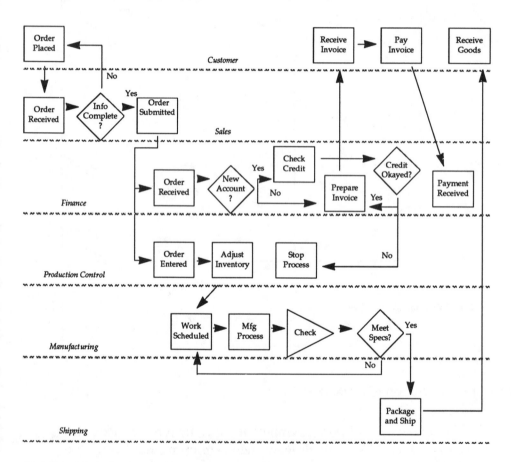

Exhibit 15-8: Order Fulfillment Process Map

Assessing and Changing the Culture

This chapter pointed out the advantages and benefits of the horizontal organization and how to make significant improvements in business processes. That's the easy part. The difficulty is getting buy-in and commitment to make the needed structural and systems changes with the appropriate breadth and depth to make a real difference. This means selling the concept to top management and ensuring the cultural barriers are adequately addressed.

Here are several tips to consider.

Tip 1 — Assess the Current Culture

Functional organizations have cultures that are well established and thoroughly reinforced by the functional structures and the systems used to make them work. The first step in any culture change effort is to identify the gap between the current culture and the ideal culture in a horizontal organization. This helps you determine the magnitude of the task you're facing. And it helps you identify the barriers that will get in the way of or dilute your efforts.

Geary Rummler and Alan Brache provide the contrasting elements of a functional and systems culture.[11] The survey in Exhibit 15-9 is adapted from their work in cultural gap analysis.

Use the survey to make an individual assessment of the organization — use the items as thought triggers to document your own perceptions. Or, ideally, get a group of people representing a cross-section of functions and levels for a more sophisticated assessment of the culture.

Read each item and rate your culture on the 7-point scale. Circle "1" if the statement on the left is a completely accurate description of your culture. Circle "7" if the statement on the right is a completely accurate description of your culture. Circle the numbers in the middle to reflect the extent that your culture is different from either extreme description.

Add the ratings across all items. If the total is less than 40, your challenge in changing the culture and introducing the horizontal organization is formidable.

Vertical Culture	Rating	Horizontal Culture
Functional needs dominate decision making.	1 2 . 3 4 5 6 7	Customer and process needs dominate decision making.
Functions interact little with one another.	1 2 3 4 5 6 7	Functions extensively interact with one another.
Most people understand only the function where they work.	1 2 3 4 5 6 7	People understand the big picture and how functions relate.
Interactions among functions tend to be confrontational.	1 2 3 4 5 6 7	Interactions among functions are collaborative.
Functional goals focus effort on narrow functional issues.	1 2 3 4 5 6 7	Goals focus on process and customer service.
A function can look good at the expense of another.	1 2 3 4 5 6 7	A function looks good only if it contributes to the whole.
Only results are measured and managed.	1 2 3 4 5 6 7	Results *and* processes are measured and managed.
Systems are examined only when there's a problem.	1 2 3 4 5 6 7	Philosophy of continuous improvement is strong.
There is little open flow of information across functions.	1 2 3 4 5 6 7	Information is shared freely across functions.
The chain of command is always strictly enforced.	1 2 3 4 5 6 7	People are encouraged to resolve issues with other functions.
Participation in decisions is confined to functions.	1 2 3 4 5 6 7	Cross-functional teams are formed to make key decisions.
People are rewarded for their functional contributions.	1 2 3 4 5 6 7	People are rewarded for their organizational contributions.

Exhibit 15-9: Culture Survey Adapted from Rummler and Brache

However, if your total is greater than 65, you'll have a rather easy time making the transition. You can use each item rating to determine the specific changes that need to occur.

Tip 2 — Get Top Management Support

It should come as no surprise that top management commitment and support is essential for a successful reengineering effort. How management allocates resources along with its own time and effort to foster team performance is the variable that dictates the destiny of the team-based organization.

McKinsey consultants Jon Katzenbach and Douglas Smith see top management's role as threefold.[12] First, they must identify which types of teams will be most effective in promoting organizational performance. Secondly, they need to know how to help accelerate the development of teamwork. Finally, they need to be aware of the issues that get in the way of team development and performance so they can anticipate and deal with them before they exert a debilitating effect.

The best way to get top management support is through education. Articles, books, visits to other organizations, and discussions with counterparts in other companies all can help top management understand the value of reengineering and how it works. This accomplished, the next step is to help them understand how the company will be better off — more competitive, efficient, and productive — why a change is beneficial and the negative consequences of not changing. Finally, a compelling concept paper can spell out how the techniques are applied in a low-risk pilot location and help move top management from curiosity to action.

Tip 3 — Define Roles for the Function Heads and Middle Managers

A major barrier to any work flow redesign is the function head and middle managers. These initiatives are threatening to function heads and middle managers because it appears that they lose authority and job security. A meaningful role in the new scheme of things must be clearly defined and sold to middle managers and function heads or they are likely to be negative about or even sabotage the plan.

Some argue that the role of the senior manager is to manage the interfaces — the white space — on the organization chart. Senior managers need not remanage the functional affairs since the boxes presumably are already staffed with competent managers.[13] Others contend that senior managers must focus more on strategic issues, leaving the day-to-day operational concerns to the middle managers. It's the middle manager's role to continually improve operational efficiency by maintaining in-depth technical understanding and "hands-on" management of the important business processes.[14]

Tip 4 — Sell, Sell, Sell

Changing the culture and paving the way for a successful reengineering effort is nothing other than a sales job. This means anticipating and addressing the differing needs of the various groups within the company and talking benefits — what's in it for them to change. Remember that most people in the company are not interested in work flow analysis, process improvement, and reengineering — the means. They are interested in results — what these initiatives will do for them and how they'll be better off if they sign on.

Selling also means thinking through the objections they are likely to raise and developing appropriate responses. Don't take objections personally. View them as valuable — signals of interest. In reality, objections are just negatively stated needs for more information.

Once the people are sold, you're ready for the fun part — implementation. You're ready to get people invigorated about the process and to empower the people who do the work to design the work. Happy work redesign.

Endnotes

1. J. Byrne. The Horizontal Corporation: It's About Managing Across, Not Up and Down. *Business Week,* December 20, 1993.

2. J. Byrne. The Horizontal Corporation: It's About Managing Across, Not Up and Down. *Business Week,* December 20, 1993.

3. J. Byrne. The Horizontal Corporation: It's About Managing Across, Not Up and Down. *Business Week,* December 20, 1993.

4. T. A. Stewart. A Master Class in Radical Change. *Fortune,* December 13, 1993.

5. G. A. Rummler & A. P. Brache. *Improving Performance: How to Manage the White Space on the Organization Chart.* San Francisco: Jossey-Bass, 1990.

6. G. A. Rummler & A. P. Brache. *Improving Performance: How to Manage the White Space on the Organization Chart.* San Francisco: Jossey-Bass, 1990.

7. M. Hammer & J. Champy. *Reengineering the Corporation: A Manifesto for Business Revolution.* New York: Harper-Collins Publishers, 1993.

8. G. A. Rummler & A. P. Brache. *Improving Performance: How to Manage the White Space on the Organization Chart.* San Francisco: Jossey-Bass, 1990.

9. M. Hammer & J. Champy. *Reengineering the Corporation: A Manifesto for Business Revolution.* New York: Harper-Collins Publishers, 1993.

10. G. Hall, J. Rosenthal & J. Wade. How to Make Reengineering Really Work. *Harvard Business Review,* November - December, 1993.

11. G. A. Rummler & A. P. Brache. *Improving Performance: How to Manage the White Space on the Organization Chart.* San Francisco: Jossey-Bass, 1990.

12. J. R. Katzenbach & D. K. Smith. *The Wisdom of Teams: Creating the High Performance Organization.* Boston: Harvard Business School Press, 1993.

13. G. A. Rummler & A. P. Brache. *Improving Performance: How to Manage the White Space on the Organization Chart*. San Francisco: Jossey-Bass, 1990.

14. L. R. Sayles. Doing Things Right: A New Imperative for Middle Managers. *Organization Dynamics*, American Management Association, Spring 1992.

Chapter

16

Leading High-Performance Teams

"No manager ever won no ballgames."
—Sparky Anderson
Baseball Manager

"She's incredible, I keep telling people. When things go wrong she takes the blame. She says it's something she failed to anticipate or communicate to us. But when things go great, it's all our doing. It's great." The enthusiasm in Jo's voice and the sparkle in her eye communicated as much as her words.

"I like her because she lets us know what she expects by being a living example of what a team player should be — not by edits and commands," John offered. "I think it's her ability to provide general guidance and then give the team autonomy to make decisions and resolve its conflicts," Dana added. "I agree," said Tim and then he continued, "and I feel strongly that she really likes people. She lets us know when we do something well and she's really concerned about helping us be the best we can. That's important in my view."

There are many descriptions of leadership traits, behaviors, strategies, and models. But what it all boils down to is this: You have to let people know what's expected — what's effective and what's not when it comes to performance. And you do this through both your words and actions. Next, you guide and facilitate the team effort by clarifying the way and removing the obstacles and roadblocks to performance. Third, you let people know how they are doing regularly — through feedback and performance data — so they know what to do more of, less of, or differently. Finally, you give people opportunities to develop and grow. Doing these things is what team leadership is all about. By doing these four things exceptionally well, your job will be easier, you will get the respect and commitment of your team members, and everyone will benefit from better business results.

James Belasco and Ralph Stayer provide insight through analogy — the head buffalo and the herd versus the flock of geese.[1] Here's the comparison, then you make the choice. Buffalo are absolute loyal followers of one leader. The head buffalo dictates what the herd will do, when, how, and where. And when the head buffalo is not around, commanding and controlling, the herd is idle, waiting for the leader to show them what to do. When told, the herd does exactly what they are instructed to do, nothing more. This is why the early settlers had such an easy time slaughtering herds. They would seek out and kill the head buffalo and the rest of the buffalo would stand around waiting for the leader to lead.

Geese, on the other hand, are interdependent, mutually supportive, and team oriented. When a flock is flying in a "V" formation, the leader is working the hardest. As you move back in the flock, the geese are buoyed by the updraft. Regularly, leadership changes all so the burden of work is equally shared. Roles of leader, follower, and scout are unselfishly rotated to the benefit of the entourage.

So this is your question: Do you want to be head buffalo or geese? If the latter is your choice, this chapter provides the tools and techniques for developing an interdependent team of people who share resources and put the team goals ahead of personal agendas.

Road Map

The *What* and *How* of Team Leadership

In defining team leadership, some researchers focus on the *what* — specific behaviors or tasks the leader displays to direct, manage, motivate, and develop team performance.

Katzenbach and Smith, McKinsey consultants, provide perhaps the most thorough definition of team leadership based on studies of hundreds of teams and nonteams.[2] They define six practices:

1. Keep a common purpose, goals, and a meaningful working approach.
2. Build commitment and confidence of each member and the team as a whole.
3. Develop a solid mix and level of skills — technical, functional, interpersonal, and teamwork skills.
4. Manage relationships with the rest of the organization and remove obstacles that can get in the way of or dilute the team effort.
5. Create opportunities for the team and the team members to make a difference — empower the team and individual members.
6. Do real work — not dirty work.

These practices are useful in describing *what* team leaders do, but the list does not fully define the *how* — the all-important style of performance. For example, the leader can develop common purpose, goals, and working approaches but do so in a way that comes across as directive, autocratic, and controlling. As a result, the team commitment to execution is low. That's why both *what* leaders do and *how* they go about it — total performance — needs to be defined.

Behavior Model of Team Leadership Patterns

Team leadership patterns — the *how* — consist of two factors, namely: *getting things done* and *building team relationships*. These factors are consistent with descriptions of leadership behavior identified in studies conducted at Ohio State University[3] and University of Michigan.[4] In addition, the factors reflect the two common categories of task- and people-related behaviors that teams and team leaders display as shown in years of research and practical application with the Dimensional Model[5] and the Managerial Grid.[6]

Action-oriented and results-driven team leaders develop missions, set challenging goals, organize roles, and structure their activities to *get things done.* Team leaders weak on this dimension are "hands-off," passive, reactive, and cautious.

Team leaders *build strong relationships* by promoting open communication, sharing resources — and by fostering active participation — while they're making decisions, solving problems, conducting meetings, or managing conflicts. Team leaders strong on this dimension are responsive to the needs and views of the members and other units with which the team interacts. Team leaders weak on this dimension are insensitive, and "me"-oriented.

This model, shown in Exhibit 16-1, further defines four distinct patterns of team leadership behavior.

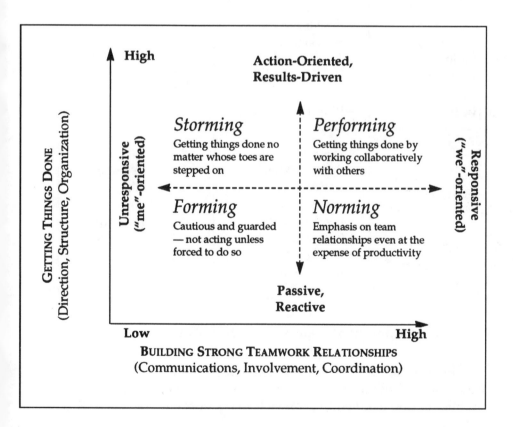

Exhibit 16-1: Team Leadership Patterns

Teamwork Pattern	Leader Behavior	Impact on Team
Forming "Don't rock the boat." "Avoid getting too involved."	• Puts off making decisions and taking action • Resists change • Withholds information	• Team members remain distant and guarded • Or, a few dominant members try to take over
Storming "I say and you do." "What can you do for me?"	• Pushes own agenda • Squelches disagreement • Punishes mistakes • Doesn't ask for input	• Team members withdraw • Low level of involvement and commitment
Norming "Let's build friendly team relationships." "Let's be friends."	• Establishes rules and boundaries • Tries to build morale and team spirit • Positive and upbeat	• Team enjoys high morale • Productivity is low
Performing "Let's work together to achieve team results." "We can achieve the best results through teamwork."	• Helps the team decide what it will achieve • Keeps people involved and informed • Lets people know how they're doing	• Team gets things done while continuously building teamwork and team member relationships

Exhibit 16-2: Team Leader and Team Member Behavior

Exhibit 16-2 shows the various teamwork patterns, team leader behavior, and the impact of each on the team. This exhibit clearly highlights one leadership approach that's effective and three that are not.

Defining Total Performance

Defining both the *what* and the *how* of team leadership is necessary to describe total performance of the team leader. To simplify the *what* of team leadership, leaders do four things:

1. *Provide Direction.* Let people know what's expected — what's effective and what's not when it comes to performance.
2. *Guide and Facilitate the Team Effort.* Do so by clarifying the path to business results and high-performance teamwork. Do so also by removing the obstacles and roadblocks that are sure to get in the way.
3. *Provide Performance Feedback.* Let people know how they are doing — through feedback and performance data — so they know what to do more of, less of, or differently as individuals and the collective team.
4. *Develop Performance and Potential.* Give people opportunities to develop and grow.

Doing these things — and doing them in a way that gets things done while building strong relationships — is what team leadership is all about.

Provide Direction

There are many tools for providing direction presented in earlier chapters. We discussed the team mission in Chapter 5 and Zest Goals in Chapter 6. In Chapter 7, we described team working agreements and in Chapter 13 we outlined strategic planning.

Framework Integrating Direction-Setting Tools

Exhibit 16-3 shows how all the tools integrate to form a system. Use this system initially to provide direction, structure, and organization for the team. Then, on an ongoing basis, use it to motivate, manage, and develop the performance and potential of the team.

Exhibit 16-3 shows the mission, which clarifies for the team its purpose, customers, and values about quality and teamwork. The team mission provides the basis for long-range planning and establishing strategic priorities to keep the focus on the long-term — a future perspective on where the team is going and ideally what the team can become. The mission also provides the basis for developing job descriptions, interim goals and objectives, and short-term Zest Goals — all of which focus the team on the short-term so people maintain a sense of urgency and excitement.

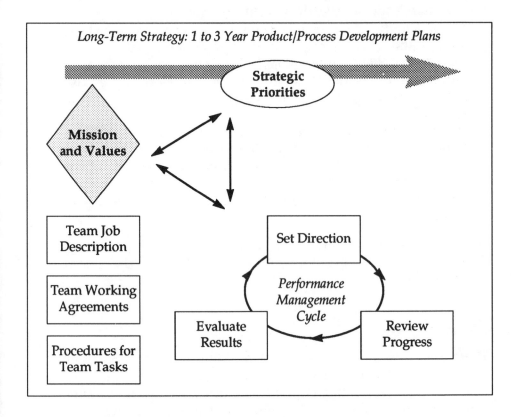

Exhibit 16-3: Framework for Providing Clear Direction

Team Goals
Exhibit 16-4 shows annual business result areas for a cross-functional product development team in a large manufacturing facility. These business results, linked to the strategic plan, are used to define short-term Zest Goals and then are translated into team member accountabilities for results. These business result areas are set by the team, consistent with the *Performing* team leadership pattern, and provide a bridge from the present to the future.

Exhibit 16-4: *Cross-Functional Product Team* Business Results Expected

Cross-Functional Product Team Business Results Expected

Each Product Team sets challenging business result targets in the following areas:

- **Financial**
  - Profit (margin objectives)
  - Production (quantity)
  - Return on Investment in Product Development

- **Customer Satisfaction**
  - Reduce Process Cycle Time
  - Meet or Exceed Specifications
  - Timely and Satisfactory Solutions to Problems (follow-up surveys)
  - Quality

The Product Teams establish business result targets, monitor performance, and coordinate with the functional units to achieve greater profitability, sounder decisions about product investments, and stronger customer satisfaction.

Team Job Description

A team job description also lets the team know what's expected — specific day-to-day responsibilities. Exhibit 16-5 shows the job description for this same cross-functional product team.

Exhibit 16-5: *Cross-Functional Product Team* Job Description

Cross-Functional Product Team Job Description

Summary of Operation and Responsibility: The Product Teams are chaired by a Product Director and consist of permanent or as-needed representatives from Manufacturing, Engineering, Finance, Materials, Marketing, and Service.

Responsible for strategic and general management of the product line, the Product Teams provide direction, solve problems, improve quality, and increase efficiency of the product line. Working collaboratively with the functions, the Product Teams perform five key functions:

1. Establish Strategic Direction for the Product Line
- Assess trends in current markets and explores new market opportunities
- Analyze competitive activity
- Define major opportunities and threats
- Identify 3-year strategic objectives showing major investments and returns
- Present objectives, strategies, and ROI figures to Management Team for approval

2. Develop Operational Plans
- Establish product business result targets supportive of strategic direction
- Develop specific work action plans with time lines and accountabilities for each Team Member
- Coordinate work action plans, time lines, and accountabilities with functional groups
- Assemble monthly income and expense forecasts and budgets
- Present targets, action plans, forecasts, and budgets to Mining Management Team for Approval

3. Manage Product Line
- Ensure that Team Members and functional departments fully understand and commit to achieving business result targets and work plans
- Meet as needed to closely monitor attainment of business result targets and adherence to action plans
- Take timely corrective action to address variances from targets, schedules, and plans
- Promote teamwork within and across functions by actively sharing information, promoting internal customer and supplier relationships, and managing conflicts and barriers to cross-functional coordination

4. Support Field Operations
- Develop promotional plans to achieve product goals
- Assist the field sales force in identifying needs, developing key account strategy, and providing technical sales presentation material
- Establish guidelines for the preparation of proposals addressing terms and conditions, pricing, and warranties consistent with the strategic and operational plans
- Support the field and sales organization with timely and thorough data, materials, service, and coordination

5. Continuously Improve Process Efficiency and Effectiveness

- Map and analyze the process work flow to determine opportunities to add value, reduce costs, cut down cycle time, and improve efficiency
- Anticipate, investigate and problem solve delays, quality problems, and other product or customer issues
- Build strong teamwork within the Team and with Functional Units by continually appraising operating effectiveness and taking action to strengthen strengths and address improvement areas

Working Agreements

Finally, clear direction means defining how the team will fit in the larger scheme of things — how the organizational systems and procedures are adapted to support teamwork — and the specific working agreements that define team norms (what's acceptable and what's not).

At the micro level, working agreements define how the team will communicate, coordinate, and work together primarily during team meetings. These are addressed in Chapter 7. If the team does not take the inititiative to develop working agreements, norms will emerge sanctioning undesirable behavior (e.g., it's all right to be 10 minutes late for meetings).

At the macro level, the team must have direction on issues like how performance will be appraised, how rewards will be allocated, and how the team will work with other units. Exhibit 16-6 shows some general, macro-level working agreements.

Exhibit 16-6: *Cross-Functional Product Team* Working Agreements (Procedures)

Selection of Team Members

Members are selected by the Product Director in consultation with the Function Head. Members are selected on the basis of technical expertise, enthusiasm, ability to work as a team, and willingness/capability to devote significant time and effort to the Team.

Role of Team Members

Team members must be committed to the product line and work cooperatively to achieve Team goals. Narrow, functional thinking must not get in the way of strategic and business decisions of the Team.

Team members serve as liaisons to and "lead workers" within the functional department — they organize resources, manage the process, solve problems, and continuously improve operating efficiency.

Team members *must* keep the functional heads and appropriate individuals within the function fully apprised of product direction, plans, problems, operations, and performance. Err on the side of too much information rather than too little.

Performance Appraisal

Each Team periodically meets to critique its performance and provide feedback to each member concerning what he/she should do more of, less of, or differently to contribute more to teamwork.

Each Team member is reviewed by the functional manager under the normal procedures except that a significant portion of overall performance is based on contribution to the Product Team. Guidelines for weighting performance on the Product Team and performance in the functional unit will be determined.

The performance of the Product Directors is determined by the achievements of the Team — their contribution to business result targets — and their attainment of additional performance targets established with the Director of Product Development and Administration.

The performance of the Director of Product Development and Administration is determined by the collective achievements of the Product Teams and attainment of other performance targets established with the General Manager.

Performance results of the Products (Product Teams) are monitored monthly.

Resolution of Performance Issues

Performance issues are addressed within the Product Teams. If the issue persists, it is elevated to the Director of Product Development and Administration, who resolves it in consultation with functional heads. Ultimately, unresolved issues may be elevated to the General Manager.

Additional Working Agreements
Additional working agreements must be anticipated and defined.

As problems occur with Product Teams and functional units, it's a signal to develop a new working agreement. This process is continuous.

Team Tasks and Activities (Procedures)

The team leader provides direction on a day-to-day basis by guiding and facilitating team tasks and activities. For example, in making decisions and solving problems, procedures are outlined for the team to follow (see Chapters 9 and 10). The team leader initiates the process by organizing the team and clarifying the procedures. Next, as the steps are carried out, the team leader ensures that things stay on track and everyone participates. Finally, at the completion of the process, the team leader conducts a process check to see if the process followed made sense in terms of getting results and promoting active participation.

Functional roles of team members are discussed in Chapter 8. These are particularly useful to the team leader during team tasks and activities. And the leader should be an effective model of functional roles.

Guide and Facilitate the Team Effort

Guiding and facilitating the team effort involves clarifying the path to business results and high-performance teamwork. The team leader must constantly be vigilant for obstacles and roadblocks that will sooner or later get in the way of teamwork. Particularly, power struggles or lack of support from other units are certain to arise.

The best way to prevent obstacles and roadblocks from interfering with team performance is to keep people informed. Regular meetings with the top management team about plans, goals, actions, and results help keep them informed and committed to the team initiatives. Then, as problems arise, the team is more likely to have the support of people that can address them.

The team leader must also be vigilant for internal team problems. Conflict and disagreement can be constructive and used to stimulate creativity. Or, it can be destructive and a source of tension and undue stress. When destructive conflict threatens the performance of the team, the team leader must intervene quickly and decisively. The lowest level of intervention is the team leader, confronting an individual outside the team to address the disruptive behavior. Moving up the intervention ladder, the team leader may confront two or more individuals outside the team setting in a conflict-resolution meeting. Or, if things persist, the leader may have to confront the issues and people in the presence of the team. Finally, a team-building session with a third party may be needed to fully intervene, get the baggage out in the open, and deal with it in a constructive way.

Provide Performance Feedback

Feedback has powerful motivational and developmental value for teams. It lets the team and the members know how they are doing so they know what to do more of, less of, or differently. Feedback can be about performance results, variances from plan, coordination with other units, customer satisfaction, or effective and ineffective behavior on the team. Depending on the type of feedback required and desired, there obviously are different sources such as internal customers, management, suppliers, and the team members themselves. But for feedback to be effective, it must be timely, specific, balanced, and candid.

Timely feedback means it is provided regularly and as close in time following the performance as is practical. For example, don't wait six months to tell a team member that he or she keeps interrupting others and finishing their thoughts for them. Ideally, the team should set aside time at least quarterly to review process — how things are working and how to correct what's not. In addition, quarterly reviews of business results or progress toward goals is appropriate in most businesses and readily available through the accounting department.

Specific feedback means just that. It specifically describes the behavior or action that was effective or ineffective along with the positive or negative consequences of continuing or discontinuing it. Praise and recognition is oftentimes given in a general way ("... outstanding report") which results in a lost opportunity to motivate the person and improve performance even more. Negative feedback is given in a way that comes across as harsh, personal, and fault-finding rather than educational, behavioral, and focusing on what should be done differently in the future.

Balanced feedback means there are both positives and negatives. Every team and team member has strengths *and* areas of improvement. To be motivating and educational, feedback must address both.

Overly positive feedback comes across as insincere and patronizing. Overly negative feedback can be debilitating rather than enabling. Make sure the team gets a good balance of both.

Finally, feedback must be candid. People must say what they really think and feel rather than what's nice, politically acceptable, and expected. Feedback that is not totally candid is of no use to the team.

Develop Performance and Potential

The very nature of teamwork makes it a tremendous developmental opportunity for the team members. Why have teams? The answer is because no one person has the skills, abilities, insights, and perspectives that are brought to bear on business issues by teams. Whenever possible, break the team's work into smaller chunks and assign it to a task force — a smaller group of team members. And when the task group is formed, make sure that it is a mixture of team members with differing skill levels. That way, the dual goals of getting things done and developing people are achieved.

Rotate team members through various tasks and assignments. For example, if the team makes monthly presentations to top management, make sure the presenting responsibility is rotated or, at least, shared. Rotating assignments to run team meetings, preparing minutes, and facilitating decision-making activities gives everyone the chance to develop and fine-tune skills, on-the-job, while the team is producing a work product.

Finally, review the performance of each team member with a focus on identifying developmental opportunities — not as a control or documentation process. As part of the review, ask team members how they can contribute more to the team and what skills they need to do so. There are many formal developmental opportunities that can be used to develop the unique needs of team members and, after the training, the team member can share the skills and techniques with the team.

Do these things and you'll get the respect of others as a true leader, facilitator, and coach. And the team will get better business results and enjoy continuous growth and development.

Establishing Planning, Performance Management, Communications Systems

To be fully effective, the team leader should establish systems for planning and performance management — systems for providing direction, facilitating performance, providing feedback, and developing potential. Exhibit 16-7 shows a schedule used by several product development teams.

In addition, communications systems should be established to keep others informed. These systems include regular reports, presentations, memos and the like distributed broadly throughout the organization. To establish communication systems, first identify the various groups in the organization — management, internal suppliers, internal customers, and other teams. Then answer two questions, what information do they *need to know* and what information would they *like to know*. Next, determine the frequency and method for getting thorough, timely, and accurate information to them and make it happen. Later, follow up to ensure they are getting the right information in the right form. Only they can be the judge of that — don't assume.

Developing and implementing systems for planning, managing performance, communicating, and developing people make the job of the team leader easier, more productive, and fun.

Product Team Activity	Frequency	Outcomes
• Strategic Planning	• Annually	• Assumptions about growth in current and new markets • Analysis of competition • 3-year strategic plan and ROI projection
• Operational Planning	• Annually	• Targets in each business result area • Work plans with timelines and accountabilities • Income and expense forecasts and budgets
• Promotional Planning	• Annually	• Sales initiatives • Market penetration activities • Cross-product selling opportunities
• Results Reviews (What's being accomplished)	• Monthly	• Progress toward business result targets • Variances from work plans, forecasts and budgets
• Team Reviews (How we're operating as a team)	• Quarterly	• Living mission and values • Quality of meetings and interactions • Actions and skills of each member
• Overall Evaluation	• Annually	• Accomplishments • Actual results versus plan

Exhibit 16-7: Schedule of Team Performance Planning and Management Systems

Endnotes

1. J. A. Belasco & R. C. Stayer. *Flight of the Buffalo: Soaring to Excellence, Learning to Let Employees Lead.* New York: Warner Books, 1993.

2. J. R. Katzenbach & D. K. Smith. *The Wisdom of Teams: Creating the High Performance Organization.* Boston: Harvard Business School Press, 1993.

3. R. Stogdill & A. Coons (Editors). *Leadership Behavior: Its Description and Measurement.* Columbus: Bureau of Business Research, Ohio State University, 1957.

4. R. Likert. *New Patterns of Management.* New York: McGraw-Hill, 1961.

5. R. E. Lefton, V. R. Buzzotta, & M. Sherberg. *Improving Productivity Through People Skills.* Cambridge: Ballinger Publishing Company, 1980.

6. R. R. Blake & J. S. Mouton. *The Managerial Grid.* Houston: Gulf, 1964.

If you have thoughts, comments or ideas about this book, I'd love to hear from you. Contact me at the following address:

Anthony R. Montebello, Ph.D.
Psychological Associates, Inc.
8390 Delmar Boulevard
St. Louis, MO 63124 USA
Phone: (314) 993-1040
Fax: (314) 993-8904